"Hamse Warfa leads with integrity and passion—whether he's serving the people of Minnesota or working with the president to improve the lives of people across the country. Warfa offers invaluable insight about the journey to becoming a great leader. I'm proud to call him an advisor and a friend."　　　　　　　　　**—TIM WALZ**, governor of Minnesota

"Hamse Warfa is a rare individual who has led successfully in the private, public, and social sectors. He knows how to bring people together across sectors to tackle problems too tough for any one sector to solve on its own. All of us can learn from the leadership lessons in his book—a distillation of the wisdom Warfa has gained in his remarkable journey from refugee to White House appointee."

　　　　　　　　—JAN RIVKIN, professor, Harvard Business School

"Hamse Warfa is a one-of-a-kind leader whose advice I've trusted for a long time. As a colleague in Minnesota state government, I got to see his leadership style up close, and he played a central role in guiding our efforts to provide economic relief to Minnesotans during the twin crises of the COVID-19 pandemic and the unrest following the murder of George Floyd. Warfa is a solutions-focused, people-centered leader with an uncanny knack for seeing the details and the big picture at the same time. I'm so glad he's putting his insights on innovative, compassionate leadership into this book, which is well worth your time."

　　　—STEVE GROVE, CEO and publisher, Minneapolis *Star Tribune*

"I met Warfa when he was a young man who had just come to the U.S. after a challenging youth of years living as a refugee in Kenya. I am honored to have developed a mentor-mentee relationship with him for almost two decades now. He has emerged as a highly respected expert on democracy, and his understanding of the value of empathy as leadership practice comes from powerful experiences. I have personally seen Warfa with world leaders, using his compassion and listening skills for great impact."　　　　　　**—CHARLES F. "CHIC" DAMBACH**,
President Emeritus, National Peace Corps Association

"A commitment to democratic participation is a central value to our lives in business, politics, and diplomacy. The story of Hamse Warfa is a hopeful reminder that the United States remains a place where a new citizen can make an incredible impact and, in Warfa's case, promote the president's democracy agenda at home and abroad."

—**AMBASSADOR SAMUEL AND SYLVIA KAPLAN,**
U.S. diplomats to Morocco

"I have founded and led successful international businesses for over fifty years. Private-sector executives need help to further develop their leadership, support their teams, and build their organizations for success. Through his example and leadership framework, Warfa can meet those business needs."

—**KJELL BERGH,** chairman, Borton Volvo

"The heart of my career has focused on bringing together business and the relief and development sectors to accomplish something neither could do on their own. It has been my experience that Hamse Warfa's asset-based approach to leadership is what the world urgently needs. Great things happen when leaders embrace their strengths and then partner with the strengths of others. In my work with entrepreneurs across Africa, I see what Warfa sees; everyone has strengths to bring toward solving our great challenges."

—**JEFF DYKSTRA,** cofounder & CEO, Partners in Food Solutions

"Warfa is an inspiring leader. He founded a global fintech business, and he understands how central accountability is to success in our ever-changing, increasingly techno-world. Warfa offers lessons in how to be an effective leader. I recommend every leader pick up this book and read; it will certainly inspire you!"

—**PHIL NOBLE,** founder, World Class Scholars

"I know Hamse Warfa as an accomplished global thought leader working across public and private sectors. There is abundance in every person, but unleashing this potential requires communities where people find belonging. I am happy to partner with Warfa and use our collective wisdom to build inclusive leadership in our communities, institutions, and governments."

—JOCELYN WYATT, CEO, Alight

"Youthprise promotes the learning, leadership, and social-emotional development of young people. Warfa's leadership accomplishments and the leadership framework described in this book provide action-oriented, practical lessons for current and emerging leaders."

—MARCUS POPE, president, Youthprise

"Hamse Warfa and I have worked together as leaders, both utilizing education as a tool for innovation in business, government, and politics. As head of Minnesota's Workforce System, Warfa collaborated with nonprofits, for-profits, and public institutions to help people access workforce training. He is an innovative leader; his book is a must-read!"

—DICK SENESE, President Emeritus, Capella University

"Throughout his career, Hamse Warfa has been a champion for transformational leadership. As the highest Somali American presidential appointee, he has been both representing Minneapolis on the national stage and helping to educate residents right here at home. I highly recommend Warfa's book, and I know readers will be inspired to take action that advances peace and prosperity."

—JACOB FREY, mayor of Minneapolis, Minnesota

"Hamse Warfa is an authentic and solutions-oriented leader—a problem solver! There is a lot to learn about leadership from his example, and this book is a much-needed guide for every leader."

—DEAN PHILLIPS, member of the U.S. Congress

"Cities across the world are tackling global issues on a local scale. Transformative leaders are needed in both the public and private sectors to confront these challenges head-on. The leadership perspective presented by Warfa in his latest book emphasizes the crucial tenets of accountability, humility, and democracy. As leaders, we can inspire positive change and pave the way for a better future."

—MELVIN CARTER, mayor of Saint Paul, Minnesota

"Hamse Warfa's remarkable American journey has taught him much about what democracy requires of citizens and those who would lead them. Warfa shares his lessons in a book chock-full of examples from his work in the Biden administration with communities from around the nation and the globe. Those lessons are gifts to anyone who wants to help democracy live up to its promise."

—LORI STURDEVANT, Minnesota journalist and author

"I've always admired people who lead with compassion. Hamse Warfa's decades of leadership and lived experience reveal how reflection and self-discovery help leaders build the skills of empathy and help people come together through understanding. I'm glad to have gotten to know Warfa over the years and know that his leadership advice has helped many people in my congressional district and around the world."

—ANGIE CRAIG, member of the U.S. Congress

"Warfa's path and accomplishments provide a roadmap for making America even greater by attracting extraordinary talent from around the globe." —R. T. RYBAK, president and CEO of the Minneapolis Foundation and former mayor of Minneapolis

THE
TRANSFORMATIONAL
LEADER

THE TRANSFORMATIONAL LEADER

Twelve Practices for Driving Lasting Change

HAMSE WARFA

WISE INK

Today, eleven tribal nations and communities are located within the state of Minnesota—the place Wise Ink calls home. Wise Ink pays tribute to the Dakota and Ojibwe as the original people of this sacred land, first called Mni Sota Makoce in the Dakota language.

Mni Sota Makoce is a place that carries a deep, layered history across the thousands of years the Dakota and Ojibwe peoples have been in kinship with the land, and in the centuries since European settlers colonized the land that the state of Minnesota now occupies. The land seizures and genocide committed by the United States were projects of spiritual and cultural destruction that denied the Dakota free and unhindered access to the land that fundamentally shapes their identity. We acknowledge that trauma has occurred, that harm continues to occur today, and that it is incumbent upon all of us residing on this land to work toward an equitable future where everyone has the opportunity to thrive. We encourage you, too, to learn and consider the history of the land on which you reside, as well as the resilient peoples and complex legacies that have made it what it is today.

ISBN 13: 978-1-63489-720-4
Library of Congress Control Number: 2024910132

Printed in the United States of America
First Printing: 2024

28 27 26 25 24   5 4 3 2 1

Cover design by Emily Mahon
Interior design by Zoe Norvell
Author photograph courtesy of the Open Society Foundation
Production editor: Amy Quale
Editor: Shari MacDonald
Proofreaders: Elizabeth Farry and Lizzie Davis

Wise Ink
PO Box 580195
Minneapolis, MN 55458
www.WiseInk.com

Wise Ink is a creative publishing agency for game-changers. Wise Ink authors uplift, inspire, and inform, and their titles support building a better and more equitable world. For more information, visit WiseInk.com.

*I dedicate this book to my paternal grandfather,
Warfa Magan Khalaf: a traditional healer, medical
expert, and wise elder who demonstrated
transformational leadership during his time.
I continue to build on his leadership legacy, and
I pray I am as useful to society as he was in his time.*

ACKNOWLEDGMENTS

I am grateful for many gifts in my life, including support from my family, mentorship from friends, and the ability to serve for two years in a presidential administration. With joy, I offer this leadership model and the stories in this book. I share them with gratitude for all those who have educated me and inspired my leadership. I pray that these words and my example contribute to a just and sustainable peace in our world.

Family

God has blessed me with a great family. My beautiful wife, Ikran Abdi, provides motivation and support as we create our life together. Our children, Samia, Subeir, Sabrina, and Suhur, make me smile, and I am lucky to be part of their growth and their futures.

I thank my mother, Hindisa (Kaltuumo), for being a leader of my family. I have many smart, successful, and caring siblings and relatives who are a consistent source of encouragement. I am forever grateful for their love and care.

Publishing This Book

Completing this book required the contributions, guidance, and mentorship of many people, some of whom I will mention here: Matt Musel, Myra Muili, Sally McGraw, John Wanjora, Tyler Zabriskie,

James Clinton, Nancy Hersage, Beirut Abafogi, Ifrah Abdullahi, Muhsin Warfa (no family relation), and Bill Graves. Amy Quale, Crown Shepherd, Hanna Kjeldbjerg, and the entire Wise Ink publishing team were great partners in shaping this book and sharing it with the world.

Colleagues

Since the publication of my last book, *America Here I Come: A Somali Refugee's Quest for Hope*, countless professional colleagues have contributed to my success as a leader and the development of this leadership model. While it is impossible to honor everyone, I want to thank the following partners.

Philanthropy

As I emerged as a leader, many philanthropic foundations invested in the work of my leadership. These include the Ashoka Foundation, the Bush Foundation, Margaret A. Cargill Philanthropies, the John and Denise Graves Foundation, the GHR Foundation, the HRK Foundation, the Justin and Susan Kelly Foundation, the McKnight Foundation, the Minneapolis Foundation, the Mortenson Family Foundation, Open Society Foundations, the Saint Paul & Minnesota Foundation, and Youthprise. I am grateful for the guidance and support I received from many as I built and maintained these relationships, especially Jane Graupman of the International Institute of Minnesota, Dana Mortenson of World Savvy, and Steve Rubin of Stinson Law.

State Government

I relied on the expertise of many in my next transition. As my career moved from philanthropy and social entrepreneurship to public service, I learned from tremendous individuals who joined me to serve Minnesota Governor Tim Walz and Lieutenant Governor Peggy Flanagan. I am grateful to individuals such as Chief of Staff Chris Schmitter, former

Commissioner Steve Grove, Pahoua Yang Hoffman, Patrick Tanis, and Nick Coe, who believed in my ability to lead Workforce Development for the state. In my three years with the Department of Employment and Economic Development, the success of my leadership was the product of thousands of state employees and regional partners who served to strengthen the state's workforce. A few of those collaborative coworkers were Ben Baglio, Blake Chaffee, Kirk Crow Shoe, Anisa Hajimumin, Lorrie Janatopoulos, Marc Majors, Abdiwahab Mohamed, Maureen Ramirez, and Huguette Trebil.

Business Partners

I am incredibly grateful for the support I received from my business partners, Ashish Gadnis and Jeff Keiser, cofounders of BanQu.

Federal Service

My two years in Washington, DC, were full of extraordinary people— colleagues in the state department, allies in the White House, and diplomats and experts from around the world. I appreciate those allies who helped me be appointed to the Biden-Harris administration: Secretary of State Tony Blinken, Under Secretary of State Uzra Zeya, and my congressional delegates, U.S. Senators Amy Klobuchar and Tina Smith and U.S. Representative Angie Craig. I am grateful to the many friends who aided my move, from those who celebrated me in Minnesota to those who helped me navigate housing and traveling around the capital. These friends include Tom Friedman, Ken Martin, Jim Deal, and Graham Faulkner; my brothers Abdirizak and Wali; my sisters Fardowsa, Kowsar, Hani, and Nasra; and my nieces and nephews, particularly Ismahan Abdullahi and Hamse Omar.

It is difficult to quantify and pay back the enormous contributions in the form of time and professional skills that all the above and other persons not listed here have invested in me. I thus wish to express my appreciation for all they have done to contribute positively to my leadership. To all those who helped me become who I am today, thank you for your love, care, and compassion.

TABLE OF CONTENTS

FOREWORD

I t is my honor to introduce you to a remarkable individual, a partner in my growth as a leader, and a good friend: Hamse Warfa. In
the realm of transformational leadership, his journey and insights
are nothing short of extraordinary. Before you proceed, I'd like to share
some of the wisdom that flows from my experiences with him and prepare you for the lessons contained within the pages of this book, *The
Transformational Leader: Twelve Practices for Driving Lasting Change*.

Let me take you back to almost ten years ago, when I received an
unexpected gift: I met Hamse Warfa. I was changing careers, leaving
behind a corporate job in project management to be the founder of
my family's charitable foundation. Like many of you, I was an emerging
leader. I was young and excited, with a big vision to change the world,
and anxious about my own leadership. Was I prepared to lead? With this
mixture of hope and doubt, I met Warfa. Only a few years older than me,
he was already an accomplished leader in his community, nonprofits,
and philanthropy. Right away, I knew that I could learn from him. He
was real, relatable, and ready to help. This same generosity is available
for you in this book.

I have experienced Warfa as a friend, a policy leader who served as the highest Somali White House appointee, and a political advisor who previously served as the highest-ranking African immigrant in Minnesota state government. When we met, he was already an established leader in international business and philanthropy, in the Minnesota nonprofit sector, and in politics in the East African community. But what impresses me most about Warfa is not his titles or professional experiences, but how easily he encourages other leaders, including me. I am a pretty quiet guy who doesn't draw attention to myself, but to achieve my vision for the Graves Foundation, I needed to continually network with new leaders and seek out new ideas. With Warfa, I got to practice an approach to partnerships that has defined my success. Together, we developed a lasting, intentional relationship as civic leaders—and with his guidance, I have become an early investor in grassroots organizations that help youth achieve thriving adult lives.

With Warfa, I have learned about power, dialogue, and transformation. It is our shared conviction that leadership is not confined only to lofty boardrooms or grandiose speeches, but also thrives in the trenches of nonprofits, classrooms, and scrappy start-ups. True transformational leadership encompasses empathy, inclusivity, and purpose-driven action. His life and work embody these principles.

Warfa's personal stories, which fill this book, are a testament to transformational potential within us all. In 2019, Minnesota governor Tim Walz appointed Warfa as the deputy commissioner leading Minnesota's Workforce Development system. He was not just a leader but the highest-ranking African immigrant official in state government, a role that placed him in a unique position to effect change. His contributions in the public sector were already significant, but they were just a part of his multifaceted life. Warfa is not a man confined to one sphere; he is a true polymath whose pursuits span public service, entrepreneurship, diplomacy, and technology.

In recent years, Warfa has become a diplomat, serving as a presidential appointee, senior advisor to the U.S. State Department. In this role, he has championed President Biden's democracy-strengthening agenda, both domestically and abroad. His commitment to fostering democratic principles, human rights, and inclusive governance is a testament to his dedication to creating a better world for all.

Yet, Warfa's influence and impact extend beyond government. He is a cofounder and executive vice president of BanQu, Inc., a pioneering for-profit/for-purpose blockchain-as-a-service software company. Through BanQu, Warfa has embarked on a mission to tackle one of the world's most pressing challenges: extreme poverty. His work with BanQu exemplifies his belief in technology as a force for good, transforming the lives of marginalized communities by enabling them to access the global economy.

As you delve into the pages of *The Transformational Leader*, you will bear witness to the wisdom, passion, and pragmatism that define Hamse Warfa. Within these pages, he distills his experiences, unveiling a blueprint for leadership that is both profound and pragmatic. He offers insights into twelve key practices that he believes should guide leaders in their quest for transformation. These practices—from inclusion and purpose to dignity and innovation—form the bedrock of Warfa's philosophy.

But what sets Warfa apart as an author and leader is not just his knowledge, but also his incredible experiences. His storytelling enlivens the subject matter, making complex ideas accessible to all. Prepare to be engaged, inspired, and occasionally amused as you journey through these pages.

As I reflect on my time spent with Warfa and our shared experiences, I am reminded of a quote from English poet and playwright William Shakespeare: "To thine own self be true." Warfa's humility and genuine curiosity embody his profound introspection. He is not a leader who claims to have all the answers; rather, he is a perpetual learner, a seeker of truths, and a champion of dialogue.

As you read this book, you will find yourself on a transformative journey guided by a leader who has walked the talk. You will discover the power of purpose, the magic of innovation, and the beauty of empathy. Warfa's words will challenge you to examine your own leadership journey, to question your assumptions, and to embrace the potential for growth and change.

After a decade of leadership of the Graves Foundation, I can see the impact of my leadership—and the impact of supporters, mentors, and friends like Warfa. Our foundation has awarded more than $15 million toward improving the lives of vulnerable young people through relationship-based grantmaking. Building on my approach to leadership—informed by Warfa—my team forms deep partnerships with local people and works with impacted communities in addressing complex social problems. As Warfa invested in me, I also invest in leadership development of youth, of nonprofits and local communities, and of my team.

As you embark on this intellectual and inspirational journey, remember that transformational leadership is not the domain of a select few; it is a calling that can be answered by anyone with the courage to lead with purpose, compassion, and innovation. Warfa is not just a guide in this endeavor; he is a living embodiment of the principles he espouses.

I am confident that *The Transformational Leader* will leave an indelible mark on your leadership journey, just as Hamse Warfa has left an indelible mark on mine. The world needs more leaders like him: leaders who are not content with the status quo, leaders who embrace diversity, and leaders who seek to uplift the human spirit. This world needs your leadership!

Sincerely,

BILL GRAVES

President
The John and Denise Graves Foundation

Becoming a Leader

People can feel the call toward leadership beginning at any age. Take me, for example. I am a former child refugee who experienced war and witnessed the death of countless innocent people after civil war broke out in Somalia in 1991. As a boy, I understood that this conflict had been caused by a failure of leadership. That was my first lesson about the important role leadership plays in the respecting of human rights and the promotion of peace. In the years since, I have lived my life as a peacebuilder: from working to contain gang violence at Crawford High School in San Diego to attending, as a diplomat representing the United States, international summits of world leaders.

To people who have never experienced violence, peace might sound like a soft word. Peace might almost seem to them to be a position of weakness. But looked at more deeply, peacebuilding can be understood to be an act of wisdom that requires both courage and strength. People who believe in peace may in fact go to any length to achieve it, not for their own sake, but for the sake of humanity.

I've begun this work by talking about leadership and peace because this book is about practicing transformational leadership that makes an impact by bringing people together to pursue good in peaceful ways: for themselves; for their families, communities, and nations; and for people everywhere.

As I learned as a child experiencing violence in Somalia, peace is an outcome of good leadership. A model of leadership will also help you create inclusive communities, economic prosperity, and a life of accountability. And inclusion, prosperity, and accountability all contribute in turn to building more peace.

As I write this book, I am serving President Joe Biden and Vice President Kamala Harris as senior advisor to the U.S. Department of State. I am the highest-ranking Somali American official to serve in a presidential administration in this country. I am honored to do this serious work, and I give 100 percent to the effort to promote inclusive democracy and an equitable economy that benefits all. But I do not work alone. The leadership model I have developed requires partnerships and is defined by listening, innovating, and organizing with others.

President Biden's intention is to restore the soul of this country, and I joined him to help advance his democracy and inclusion agenda. Like President Biden, I practice empathy as a key leadership practice. I am moved by the pain and suffering of people. I'm far from the only one who is. All across the Biden-Harris administration there are public servants like me who demonstrate innovation in leadership by listening to the lived experiences, the real stories, of people. Using what we learn, we work together to help our government do better. Purpose, empathy, innovation, and democracy are essential values for leaders who want to practice effective actions.

I do this work because I believe it's important, and leadership skills are important to doing my job well. But my job is not what makes me a leader. My father was a businessman, and he was a leader. My wife is a mother, and she is a leader. I know schoolteachers who are leaders. I know janitors who are leaders. I know artists who are leaders. Anyone can be a leader, and leaders are needed everywhere. As speaker and thinker John C. Maxwell writes in *The 21 Indispensable Qualities of a Leader: Becoming the Person Others Will Want to Follow*, "Everything rises and falls on leadership."

A RETURN TO MY HOMETOWN

Having successfully led as a Black man, a Muslim, and a Somali refugee, across multiple public sectors—as well as having created my own businesses focused on economic justice—I know what it takes to be a transformative leader in today's challenging and dynamic environment. This is the knowledge that I wish to transfer to you. When I embody the principles I teach, I make a difference. By sharing my leadership as a guide with others, I am living within my life's purpose.

So allow me to start with a story: one extraordinary experience that integrates all twelve of my leadership practices. This story is profoundly personal for me and demonstrates the four levels of leadership that I talk about in this book: self, team, organization, and community. It also illustrates my continued growth as a leader.

LEADING FROM SELF: INTEGRITY, PURPOSE, AND ACCOUNTABILITY

After I'd been away from Somalia for thirty years, I found myself considering a return visit to Mogadishu in August 2023. I had long felt the pull to return. Leadership, both in work and in life, begins in making a commitment, and I was uncertain at first about whether or not I should go. At the time, I was working in Washington, DC, for the Biden administration. My wife and children were in Minnesota. This decision to take three weeks away from both my job and my family was a big sacrifice.

I was also a little scared. I had been a preteen boy when my family fled the bullets and bombs of the Somali Civil War. Somalia is much safer today, but every choice has risks.

I considered my commitments to family, work, and safety. I also weighed my values. I tell people that I am a peacebuilder, and I felt a visit to Mogadishu was what a peacebuilder with strong personal ties to this city would do. This meant that the question of traveling to Somalia became in part an issue of my **integrity**.

The big choices in my life are never about my opinion alone, however. The most effective leader is purpose-driven, and I have learned that I can better understand my **purpose** through talking with people I trust.

I knew that I needed to share my ideas for a visit to Somalia and learn from the reactions of my family, friends, and coworkers. When I did so, I heard many different thoughts. Some people discouraged me from taking the trip, and I listened to their concerns. But my wife supported me and offered to take even greater responsibility for our children in my absence. My boss supported me and allowed me time away from work for this personal trip. My family in Kenya and Somalia, especially my brothers, offered to organize details and plan events. This assistance from trusted partners helped me feel confident in making my decision.

At this point I was excited about the trip, and my family was excited too. But excitement alone is not leadership. As a leader, I felt it was important to integrate leadership into my travel experience. How would I make the most out of the visit? What did I have to offer the people of Somalia?

After much thought, I decided that my return to Mogadishu would include a public conversation about leadership. I connected with a Mogadishu-based think tank that agreed to host this conversation and recruit emerging leaders, including young adults and women leaders, to join me. I would be returning not as a tourist or as a diplomat but to share my model of transformational leadership. A leader is **accountable** for their decisions, and my visit to Somalia would create new relationships for me with these emerging leaders. If my leadership conversation was successful, I would be part of their futures, and they would hold me accountable for my future leadership.

LEADING WITH TEAMS: DIGNITY, EMPATHY, AND INCLUSION

On Wednesday, August 2, I flew from Washington, DC, to New York and then to Nairobi, Kenya, where I had arranged to rest for a day after the fourteen-hour flight. I needed to stay healthy and adjust to the changes in time zones. Although I had a safety plan for my visit to Somalia, I was nervous about safety on this trip: not just mine, but also the safety of those I would be meeting. While I was going for personal reasons, not as a representative of the United States government, I knew that the purpose of my travel did not ensure security; political violence occurs in parts of Somalia, and there are people who identify the United States as the enemy. I respect the **dignity** of every human being, starting with safety as a basic human right.

How do I describe the emotions I felt upon landing in Mogadishu? I was greeted at the airport by leaders of government and business. I was welcomed home by family and friends. There were traditional dancers present who brought festival color and energy to my arrival, and television cameras and reporters were there to record the moment.

I was greeted with handshakes, warm smiles, and words of celebration, and I felt deeply connected to those surrounding me. I was eager to listen, to learn, and to be with the people of Somalia. While the formal ceremony of their welcome made me feel important, my heart called me to draw closer. During my visit, I surrendered my pride and chose to center my efforts on feeling **empathy**. While the attention I'd received was enjoyable, I knew that leadership is about more than feeling good. Leadership requires being meaningfully present in order to experience and hear the needs of others.

My conversation on leadership, youth, and diaspora was a huge success. More than three hundred emerging leaders, both men and women, gathered at a hotel ballroom to talk with me. (Over seven thousand had registered, but the space could only accommodate a fraction of that number.) I shared some wisdom, emphasizing that lessons learned from today's obstacles can become the foundation for future success. I also listened intently to these young adults: to their hopes and dreams for their lives and for the future of Somalia.

I focused on youth because the leadership of young people is necessary for the prosperity of every society, but they often are excluded from important conversations. The world is always changing, and to succeed in the midst of change, leaders need to be **inclusive**: open to new ideas and to new people joining their teams. These emerging leaders made me feel welcome in Somalia, and I hope my words and my spirit helped them feel included in the event.

LEADING IN ORGANIZATIONS: ASSETS, INNOVATION, AND PROSPERITY

Somalia is a country where arid deserts meet the ocean. It also has the longest coastline on the continent of Africa. The point where the sand meets the water is the setting for many joyful memories from my boyhood, and following my leadership conversation in Mogadishu, I traveled to the Somali state of Jubaland, to the pristine Kismayo beaches I remembered from my early years.

Resting at the beach, I reflected on my diverse set of strengths and considered what my leadership could build. A leader must examine the strengths and weaknesses of any situation, and the best leaders are **asset-based** and build on their strengths. My father did this. He grew up in a nomadic community, tending to cattle and camels that roamed the natural landscape for nutrients. Later, he built an international company that traded livestock, using the Somali coastline as a port to ship cattle around the region.

I could see some of my strengths: my reputation as a successful manager of complicated projects in business, nonprofits, and government; my relationships with investors, philanthropists, and members of the U.S. government from the White House to local agencies. These were all assets within my model of leadership. But a leader cannot build something new alone. Luckily for me, the next stop of my journey included a luncheon with **innovative** business leaders in Nairobi, Kenya.

Nairobi is a regional center that connects the most creative entrepreneurs across East Africa, and there, I discussed with others new business solutions for real-life problems of people in the region. At the lunch, I looked for opportunities to collaborate with other leaders and to bring together a diverse set of strengths. I again listened to the voices of women and young people whose different lived experiences contribute to the generation of unique ideas.

My conversations focused on the importance of social impact in leadership. By that I mean that leaders should benefit from their efforts, but society must also benefit. Transformative leadership is a model that builds shared **prosperity**. In the state of Minnesota, there is a well-known saying coined by the late senator Paul Wellstone: "We all do better when we all do better." This is the underlying principle behind one question we discussed at the gathering in Nairobi: the world is rich with human and natural resources, and some industries are experiencing exponential growth, but are the fruits of this growth shared ethically?

When I returned to Mogadishu, I was welcomed by Somalia's prime minister, and we discussed our shared passion for the economic revitalization of East Africa. I shared with him, and with others I met during my visit, my belief that the peace and prosperity of any region is created by trustworthy public servants who are accountable to the people of the democracy and who lead with integrity.

LEADING FOR COMMUNITY: HUMILITY, DEMOCRACY, AND PEACE

Rookie. Scam artist. Useful idiot. Devil. These are some words that people on Twitter used to describe me during my visit to Somalia. One called me an "enemy," and another said that I must be arrested. None of these words were pleasant to read. But freedom of speech lies at the heart of democracy, and these verbal attacks are a symbol of democracy.

Authoritarian leaders do not allow dissent. Quite the opposite: they use physical violence in response to verbal attacks. Leaders of free people, on the other hand, must practice **humility**. As a public servant in the Biden administration, I understand that many passionate and good people object to various aspects of the United States' leadership and policy. I also know that I am not a perfect leader. Sometimes a leader needs to stand in the middle of a conflict, and sometimes one's leadership will fail to meet the moment. It takes courage to be vulnerable as a leader.

My visit to East Africa tested my skills as a leader for democracy because democracy itself challenges its champions, in the U.S. and elsewhere, to live according to its ideals. In addition to the previously mentioned conversations I had in Mogadishu and Nairobi, I also contributed to leadership conversations with leaders in two other cities in Somalia: Kismayo and Garowe, in the federal member states of Jubaland and Puntland. During these conversations, I encouraged leaders to come together and make powerful demands of their government. A healthy **democracy** requires people to organize and to petition their elected and appointed leaders to make needed changes.

In addition to meeting members of the younger generation that is hungry to build a prosperous future, I met some senior leaders who had personally benefited from the status quo and who were cautious about democracy and human rights. My travel was personal in nature, and I could not speak to them on behalf of the United States government, but I did share my belief in democracy with them. That belief includes my conviction that leaders in a democracy must be humble enough to be challenged. Importantly, leaders must in turn come together to challenge corruption and unfair practices. I hope that the content of my talks in East Africa and in the chapters of this book help people organize collectively for the common good.

During my trip, I also had the unique opportunity to meet members of the U.S. armed forces who were part of the United States Africa Command (AFRICOM), stationed at the airport in Kismayo, Jubaland, to assist the Somali National Army in its continued fight against the militant group Al-Shabaab. I thanked these members for their service, speaking as an American and as a leader of Somali origin. In addition to meeting them, I was excited to spend time with colleagues at the U.S. embassies in both Mogadishu and Nairobi.

All of these events gave me much to contemplate. But my final thoughts on this trip were of my parents: my late father, Mohamed, who passed away at the start of the Somali Civil War, and my mother, Hindisa (a.k.a. Kaltuumo), who lives in San Diego, where my siblings take turns living with her. Over my twenty days of visiting East Africa, I thought of them, and of all they lost when we left our home. They sacrificed to save our family from war, and to find peace. Both my parents had been successful businesspeople in Somalia, and they had hoped that good jobs and economic success would provide safety for our family. Wealth, however, does not guarantee **peace**.

I understood this even as a child. On our last day in Mogadishu in 1992, I left my family briefly to join a peace march made up of young people. At that young age, I already believed that civic leadership was fundamental to long-term peace. I pray now that my 2023 visit contributed positively to the stability of Somalia and that in my words and actions, I demonstrated transformational leadership in practice.

The Transformational Leader
12 Practices for Driving Lasting Change

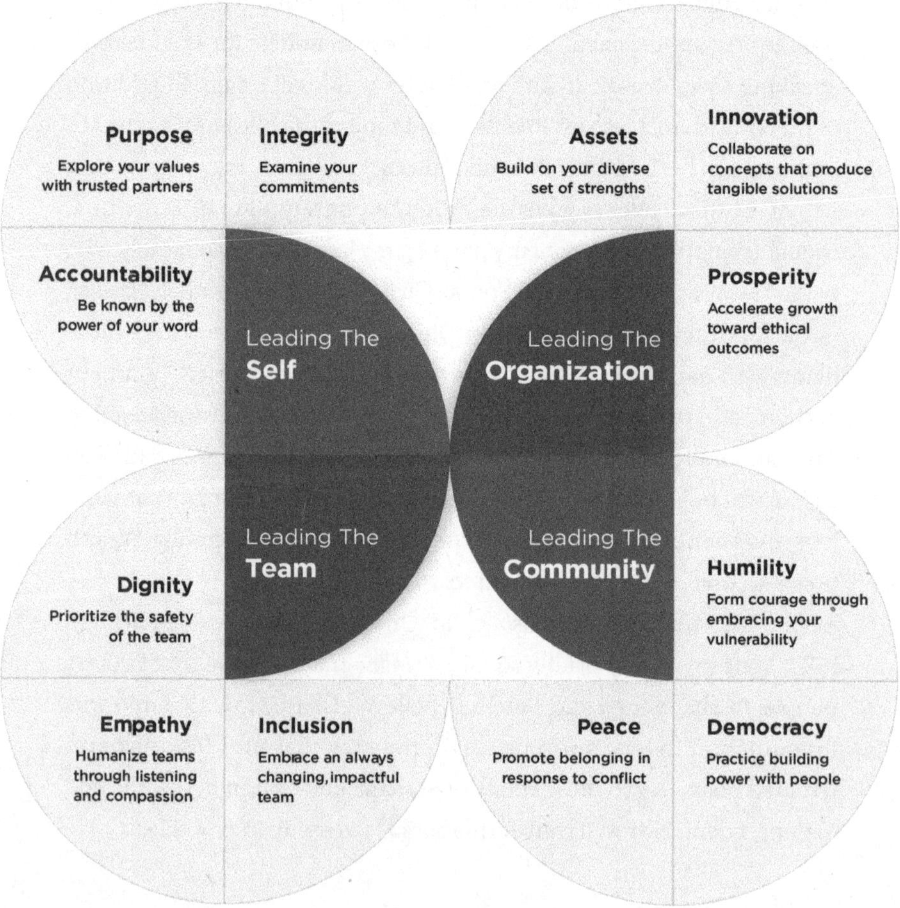

Purpose
Explore your values with trusted partners

Integrity
Examine your commitments

Assets
Build on your diverse set of strengths

Innovation
Collaborate on concepts that produce tangible solutions

Accountability
Be known by the power of your word

Leading The Self

Leading The Organization

Prosperity
Accelerate growth toward ethical outcomes

Leading The Team

Leading The Community

Dignity
Prioritize the safety of the team

Humility
Form courage through embracing your vulnerability

Empathy
Humanize teams through listening and compassion

Inclusion
Embrace an always changing, impactful team

Peace
Promote belonging in response to conflict

Democracy
Practice building power with people

THE PURPOSE OF THIS BOOK

The story I just shared illustrates an important time of leadership in my life, and the fact that you're reading these words shows that this is the right time for you to focus on leadership. The transformative leadership model outlined in this book focuses on the goal of sustained and inclusive prosperity, achieved by aligning leadership of the self, the team, the organization, and the larger community. My hope for this book is that it will develop, cultivate, and empower leaders like you through its focus on the values of integrity and purpose, and on the work of building safe, dynamic, and inclusive teams that are equipped to achieve asset-based innovation.

I use this book to share with you my lived experiences as a child refugee, senior leader in government, business and nonprofit founder, executive, and global thought leader. I also call on principles of academic theory and traditional wisdom to help you learn from peacebuilding, democratic participation, and the practice of vulnerability. The book focuses on actionable ways you can engage in the democratic process, and it also shares knowledge and inspiration to act that can be used by individuals, families, neighborhoods, organizations, and communities. I am blessed by the fact that my leadership has made a difference, and if you also want to respond to urgent needs with leadership that serves the greater good, this book is for you.

As the founder and CEO of the Warfa Foundation, and as a founder and leader in multiple businesses as well as in complicated government bureaucracies in local and federal governments, I have used the lessons of this book to build teams and transform organizations. When I picture the potential benefit of these teachings, I see a future that is inclusive, innovative, and prosperous, and that is made possible by empowering leaders to be transformational, values-driven change agents who find tangible solutions within intangible challenges, and who leverage opportunity for change.

Leaders formed in this transformational model are asset-based and empathic, and they treat individuals with dignity. It is my intention to train over ten thousand people across the world with this model over the next decade, starting in my homes in East Africa and the United States.

That figure also includes readers in every location. If you are an emerging leader rooted in integrity and purpose, and if you're eager to find new strategies to make your work even more impactful, this book is for you. Across the globe, we are in a moment of historic generational change in leadership. In the United States, for example, 75 percent of all those who run S&P 500 companies are between fifty-nine and seventy-seven years old, and they control over half of the nation's wealth. In the next ten years, the majority of these executives will retire.

This generational leadership change impacts the public sector as much as it does the private sector. By 2026, 85 percent of the senior executive service—top career officials in the federal government—will be eligible for retirement. Each day, an average of ten thousand people retire.

This shift will create a critical and expanding absence of leadership across the public and private sectors, as well as a profound opportunity to ensure the rising generation of leaders transforms existing democratic and economic systems to achieve more equitable and prosperous systems. I pray that this book can help you lead in a transformative way, with exponential impact.

PART I

Leading the Self

Personal leadership is the foundation of successful team, organizational, national, and global leadership, and fostering such leadership starts with the pursuit of self-awareness and emotional intelligence. That is to say, by leading the self. This entails developing a deep understanding of one's strengths, weaknesses, values, and emotions, as well as working on a continuous improvement program. I have learned that as a leader, I must be able to regulate my emotions, empathize with others, and effectively manage relationships. Doing so enables me to understand the vulnerabilities and needs of the people I lead, and to engage them positively in the development of effective solutions to the problem of how to get these needs met.

One of the first leaders I remember observing was my paternal grandfather, Warfa Magan Khalaf: a traditional healer, medical expert, and wise elder who stayed in our large family home in Mogadishu. I was a small boy then, and he was approaching one hundred. His lifespan had coincided with a period of epic changes in East Africa: democratic independence, global and colonial wars, and the colonization of historically indigenous lands.

He had grown up among grazing camels, goats, and sheep, in a traditional nomadic community where leadership was connected to nature. Such communities were self-sufficient networks that were deeply connected to the land, the animals, and all of vegetative life. This is likely where he was first introduced to the tools of healing: herbal remedies, prayers, and fire-burning. Plants provided herbs for healing teas and salves. Fire and tree branches were used for intense heat to cure illness. My grandfather learned all this from his elders, who had themselves learned from a previous generation of elders.

As would happen years later to my father, and later still to me, my grandfather was displaced from his home in the Ogaden region under Ethiopia at a young age. Fleeing the violence of the colonizers, he traveled across the Horn of Africa—what is now Somalia, Ethiopia, Djibouti, Eritrea, and Kenya—and eventually made it all the way to Yemen, across the sea, on the Arabian Peninsula. There, his study of the Quran, the holy book of the Islamic faith, led him to become a religious leader, and his interest in modern medicine, especially internal medicine, made him into a medical expert. Without attending a formal school, by observing doctors at work, he learned how to treat lung disease. He watched them perform surgeries and learned to perform them himself.

Later, after he returned to the nomadic community of his youth, my grandfather led his people as a healer. People came to him for care from across Somali territories and beyond. Because of his specialized modern training, he was able to teach other healers to cure lung illnesses and treat other internal diseases. He made a difference in our family and in the lives of many across the region.

My grandfather's leadership served his faith, his family, and his needs, but many leaders seek to excel in team, organizational, and community leadership at the expense of their personal and their families' well-being. They don't see that this also creates a failure in their overall leadership. While they may be good at listening empathetically to the needs of colleagues, work teams, and the communities they lead, they fail to do the same at home: the very place where their most important social support system can be found.

I have always been ambitious, striving to excel in my career while also nurturing my personal life. However, I learned early on that I needed to be deliberate in my efforts to achieve equilibrium between my professional and personal spheres. I don't want to end up burning out or missing out on the simple joys of life.

To achieve this equilibrium, I have had to establish clear boundaries between work and personal time. I have learned to be more assertive in communicating both my availability and my limitations to my team and colleagues. I have found that when I set realistic expectations, people respect my boundaries and are more considerate of my time.

I have also had to learn to prioritize self-care. At one point, I began waking up early to engage in activities that brought me joy and relaxation, such as prayer, meditation, and exercise. These morning rituals not only energize me but also set a positive tone for the rest of the day. I am also mindful of my dietary choices and make sure to fuel my body with nutritious foods. I have further implemented something known as "digital detox" periods during weekends; during these times, I refrain from checking work-related emails or messages, allowing myself to be fully immersed in leisure activities, quality time with my loved ones, and hobbies that give me joy.

Another pivotal aspect of maintaining balance is learning to delegate and trust one's team. In my own life, I came to realize that I don't have to shoulder all the responsibilities on my own. By empowering my colleagues and distributing tasks effectively, I not only reduce my workload but also foster a sense of ownership and growth among my team members.

Leaders must keep a clear view of their commitments, stay on purpose, and remain accountable. They need to set boundaries, prioritize self-care, and create routines that promote balance and sustainable performance. Effective personal leadership can be built on three principles: integrity, purpose, and accountability. These principles will be the focus of the first section of this book.

PRACTICE 1

Integrity

JOINING THE BIDEN-HARRIS ADMINISTRATION

In January 2021, President Joe Biden called for an official Year of Action to support democratic renewal across the globe, to follow the first Summit for Democracy that took place in December 2021, in which over one hundred government, civil-society, and private-sector leaders around the world participated. In response to an invitation to apply to become a presidential appointee, I joined the Biden administration as a senior advisor and presidential political appointee to the U.S. State Department. It is truly an honor and life-changing experience for me to serve with some of the most diverse, talented, and committed public servants in the U.S. federal government, working with them to advance inclusion and democracy both at home and abroad.

This is yet another opportunity that has come out of my lifelong commitment to serve as a leader and out of a promise I had made to myself as a teenager to be useful to society. I had made these pledges to myself, to my children, and to my community, whose lives had been put on the line years earlier, when the previous administration under Donald Trump made us out to be the enemy to America and weaponized our identity.

These commitments were not made on the spur of the moment. True, time had since cemented them, but their origins go deeper and further than my appointment to President Biden's administration. They touch on a loyalty to my values. They are part of a journey that started under my father's influence, when I was young. In fact, one of the things I remember best about my father, who passed away in the early 1990s during my tender preteen years, is his special prayer.

MY FATHER'S SPECIAL PRAYER

This story begins in a time long before the winds of chaos swept through my homeland of Somalia: a time when peace still dwelled within the hearts of the people, when I was just a boy growing up in Mogadishu. Back then, in the 1980s, the land was fertile, and life flowed with simplicity and harmony.

My father, Mohamed Warfa Magan, was a man of great wisdom and gentle strength. To my young eyes, he seemed to live out a unique prayer that he made every morning: a prayer that held a special place in his heart, shaped every one of his decisions, and inevitably became a driving force in my life too. It is a prayer that carried the hopes and dreams he had for his children, and it is a prayer that reminds me of my own commitments. This prayer is simple but profound: "May I be useful to society and may you be useful to society."

As a child, I often sat with my father, watching the last rays of sunlight disappear into the horizon. I remember how my father's voice resonated with a sense of purpose and devotion. Everything he said sounded important. I would listen intently, eager to understand the true meaning behind his words.

One evening, curiosity overwhelmed me, and I summoned the courage to ask my father about his childhood. He smiled tenderly and beckoned me to sit beside him. His eyes, filled with memories of a different time, met mine.

"Son," he began, his voice carrying the weight of experience, "my childhood was not easy, but it made me who I am today."

He explained that at a young age he had fled the Somalia-Ethiopia conflict of the 1960s and 1970s, traveling over the disputed Ogaden region in Ethiopia. This meant he had been forced to walk for two months to reach Somalia.

Years later, when I found myself in a confused haze as I escaped the burning city of Mogadishu, heading to a refugee camp hundreds of miles away in Kenya, that experience gave me much greater appreciation and compassion for my dad. It allowed me to fill in some of the gaps in his stories that, because of my privilege at the time, had been difficult for me to understand. It helped me connect to the universality of suffering, to its meaninglessness when its teachings are left unharnessed, and to the lesson that my father seemed to have drawn from his own suffering: that people are not solitary beings, but rather interconnected threads in the fabric of society. Being useful to society is a call to find our purpose, our unique gifts, and use them for the greater good.

He had been just a boy when his family, like many others, found themselves caught in the cross fire of the Somalia-Ethiopia conflict. The Ogaden territory had become a battleground, the fighting tearing families apart and shattering the tranquility that once enveloped their lives. With each passing day, the violence escalated and the situation grew increasingly perilous.

Faced with imminent danger and the uncertainty of what lay ahead, my father made the difficult decision to go in search of safety and refuge. The journey was a grueling test of endurance and resilience. He traversed treacherous terrains, enduring scorching sun and biting cold alike. Hunger gnawed at his belly, and thirst parched his throat. Every step was a battle against fatigue and despair, yet he pressed on, fueled by a determination to survive.

I imagine that during those two months, my dad witnessed scenes that would forever be imprinted on his mind. Families huddled together for warmth, weary with exhaustion that etched their faces, yet never losing hope. Children, their laughter silenced by the harsh reality, trudging along with a quiet resilience that belied their tender years. I can picture these things because this was exactly my experience as a teenager—the main differences being that I traveled to a different destination and I made my journey in the company of family members, all of us united by our suffering.

On his journey, my dad discovered the depths of his strength and resilience. With no money, no support, and no place else to turn, he had to seek refuge at a mosque where he knew no one. This forced him to learn to interact with strangers, a skill that would serve him well when he later became an entrepreneur. After a few months at the mosque, he secured a job with a trader who exported livestock to the Middle East and other parts of the Horn of Africa region, and he worked for this trader for several years until he had saved enough to start his own business as a livestock trader. In time, my father met my loving and beautiful mother, Hindisa (a.k.a. Kaltuumo) Hassan Seed. With her support and encouragement, he grew his company steadily into a large livestock trading company. This is where my family's business success started.

But in my youth, I did not know my father as the excellent businessman that he was, not really. At home, though we enjoyed the fruit of his hard work, he was simply a dad. He was there. He was present when we needed him. Exactly how he managed to both run a successful business and lead a large family still eludes me, but I learn from his example every day and strive to emulate it.

If there is something that everyone in my family remembers him for, it is his belief that education is the key to a successful life. I do not only mean formal school education here. My father valued an education of the self. He believed that true self-awareness lays the foundation for good leadership.

I agree. It is my experience that self-awareness forms the basis for effective communication, emotional intelligence, and decision-making. Self-aware leaders have a clear understanding of their strengths and weaknesses. This awareness enables them to leverage their strengths effectively and to seek support and opportunities for development in areas where they are less proficient. It promotes authenticity and transparency, which are qualities that followers appreciate in their leaders.

Though my father couldn't enjoy the pleasure of studying much himself, he was candid about his belief that times had changed and that the economic fortunes of his generation wouldn't be of much use to his children unless we went to school, worked hard, and became what we wanted to be in life. He was convinced that our biggest assets were not anything we had, but rather who we were, and that this was the advantage we needed to leverage. He thus ensured that my siblings and I all gained the highest quality of education possible. He also helped my mother establish a successful clothing retail business in Mogadishu, which she ran for twenty-five years, until the war broke out in 1991.

On account of my dad's flourishing import and export business and my mom's retail store, my family lived quite comfortably in an affluent part of Mogadishu. Our house sat on a large compound and was structured like the single-family homes built in the United States in the 1980s. It was a single-story building with eleven rooms. More walkways were paved in our neighborhood than in others, and its driveways were some of the best in the city: facts that, given third-world standards at that time, were worth noting.

Thinking back now, I see that my father was a man of integrity. He knew where his limits lay, and he communicated them honestly. When he made a promise, he honored it. Those who knew him knew that they could rely on him.

We kids also knew that we had to get a good education. Dad would not have it any other way. For me, the quest for education would always be tied to a quest for self-understanding. This was true even later on in life. This pursuit was driven by many factors, and it was a fight I waged against many odds. But always, it was about leveraging myself as my biggest asset. I knew that I had to live true to my late father's vision for me. He had always wanted his children to live a good life, and I believe a good life is a life of integrity.

WALK IN INTEGRITY

From my father, I learned that good leaders have to walk in integrity. The only way to figure out whether that's what one is doing is by looking inside. Integrity refers to the quality of being honest, trustworthy, and morally upright. It involves adhering to a set of ethical principles and values, and consistently acting by them, even when doing so is difficult or unpopular. People who exhibit integrity are considered to be reliable, dependable, and principled.

Integrity is widely thought to be a fundamental aspect of good character and is highly valued in many cultures and professions. It is particularly important in the field of leadership, where people who exhibit integrity are more likely to gain the respect of others. Leaders with integrity are seen as being honest and fair, and this helps them to build strong relationships with their team members and other stake-holders. Integrity is also the foundation of trust. When you consistently act with integrity, others perceive you as trustworthy and reliable, which builds credibility and fosters strong relationships, both in your personal life and professionally.

Knowing and honoring your commitments often makes life simpler in a world where there are so many demands on a person's time and so many opportunities to do great things. When I honor my commitments, I remember who I am. I think about how my father did it: when deciding between a number of choices, he used to ask himself, "What makes me useful to society?" That practice helped him to return to himself and to what he valued. It does the same for me.

Building my integrity by being useful to society helps people trust me. Grounding my integrity in a desire to do good for others helps me naturally gravitate toward making ethical decisions. When I'm faced with dilemmas, integrity helps me make decisions that are principled, fair, and morally sound. Upholding my integrity helps ensure that my actions are consistent with my beliefs and contribute to the greater good.

In professional circles, a person's integrity significantly influences their reputation and personal brand, which opens growth opportunities. Employers and customers value individuals with strong ethical standards, as they can be trusted to act in the best interest of the organization and customers. This trust becomes the foundation for the person's long-term success and well-being.

Based on the description above, we see that integrity is a hallmark for effective leadership. Leaders who demonstrate integrity inspire and motivate others. By consistently acting with honesty, transparency, and ethical conduct, leaders gain the trust and loyalty of their teams, fostering a positive work culture, and increasing team productivity and collaboration.

EXAMINE YOUR COMMITMENTS

Over the years, I have reflected on the lessons I learned from my dad. When I realized I had to be intentional about setting aside time away from work for my family, I also realized what an exemplary man my father had been. While I appreciate the opportunity I have to build bridges, promote democratic understanding, and advocate for peace, I dare not forget this example of integrity that I first saw demonstrated by my father. When I am in those moments of service, I see that the true power of my father's prayer rests in my ability to figure out my priorities and walk in integrity even in the most challenging circumstances. Years after witnessing him pray that prayer—as I stand on foreign soil, far from the land that birthed me—I carry my father's prayer in my heart. Though Somalia still struggles to heal its wounds, I remain committed to being useful to society at a global level. I advocate for peace, education, and progress, channeling the resilience I inherited from my father.

Following his example, I am passing on to my children my commitment to self-knowledge and personal growth, and I hope to exemplify integrity in how I live my life. Because of my unique vantage point—as someone who is deeply rooted in the U.S. as a parent and community leader, and who is also engaged deeply in communities across the world—I want to offer you my thoughts on the state of our global village: both the opportunities and, frankly, the challenges we face as leaders and parents as we prepare our young people to be productive global citizens.

Kids today are growing up in a completely new reality. The pace of change is ever increasing, the amount of information available is greater than in any previous generation, and it is continuing to grow at an exponential rate. If you look at the news headlines about global affairs from a big-picture level, it seems the world is falling apart, with sound bites emphasizing the incredible amount of human suffering around the world. We are also living at a time when many things seem disturbing, foreshadowing gloom and doom. We have to figure out a way to pass on our values in this kind of global landscape.

As a father of four young children, some of whom are beginning to come to an awareness of their multicultural and complex identity, I know that teaching them about integrity is the best way to ensure that their gifts and perspectives are cemented in truth and can be lived out throughout their lives. Like any parent, I want my children to thrive in the world. I want them to be useful in twenty-first century society. I want them to feel seen and heard, and to see and hear others. This has been my lifelong commitment: bringing my children up in such a way that these things would be a reality for them.

I see the principles of walking in integrity play out everywhere I look. Jeff, a sales leader in a New York–based real estate company and a close friend, tells me that in the field of sales you're only as good as the last deal you closed. Interestingly, the same is true of integrity. In life, you're only as trustworthy as the last trustworthy deed that you've done. Building integrity is, therefore, a lifelong commitment that requires self-reflection, self-discipline, and a commitment to living by your values and principles every day.

Here are some steps you can take to build integrity:

1. Be consistent.

Strive for consistency between your words, actions, and beliefs. Act in a manner that reflects your values consistently, even in challenging situations. Avoid compromising your principles for short-term gains or convenience. By being consistent, you will become trustworthy in the eyes of others. Always keep your commitments and promises.

2. Discipline yourself.

Cultivate the self-discipline to resist temptations, and strive to make ethical choices, even in challenging circumstances. Develop the habit of considering the potential consequences of your actions before making decisions. While you're at it, discipline yourself in terms of the people you allow to surround you. You want most of your interactions to be with individuals who value integrity and uphold similar ethical standards to yours. Engage in communities, organizations, and relationships that promote and support integrity.

3. Celebrate completed commitments.

When you follow through on a promise you've made to yourself or to others, celebrate it. Recognize that your honoring of commitments is a reflection of your integrity. Take a moment to acknowledge your achievements, whether they're big or small. This positive reinforcement underlines the importance of sticking to your word and helps you build a sense of pride in your integrity.

4. Recommit to commitments that move you.

Not all commitments are created equal. Focus most on the ones that truly resonate with your values and aspirations. These commitments align with your passions and drive, making it easier for you to maintain your integrity. When you're enthusiastic about what you're doing, you're more likely to stay dedicated and deliver on your promises. Regularly recommit to these important goals, to keep your integrity strong.

5. Clean up past incomplete commitments.

Sometimes life gets in the way, and commitments can fall by the way-side. Don't let these past incompletions define your integrity. Instead, take responsibility for them. Reach out to those affected by your unfinished commitments, and communicate your intentions to rectify the situation. Apologize if necessary, explain your circumstances, and make amends. Tying up past loose ends not only demonstrates your integrity, it also clears a path for you to make more meaningful commitments in the future.

6. Follow through on your promises.

Following through on promises demonstrates reliability, integrity, and respect for your commitments. It is an ongoing process that requires dedication and discipline. When you consistently honor your commitments, you strengthen your reputation, foster trust in your relationships, and cultivate a reputation for being reliable and dependable. Of course, becoming highly dependable requires that you start by not making more commitments than you can keep, and that you continue by fulfilling the promises you do make, which is where the first item in this section comes in. Consider the potential challenges and potential impact on others, and determine whether what you are about to take up aligns with your values and capabilities.

One challenge to consider is: How will you follow through on your promises? Since following through on promises is so important to leading with integrity, let's dive a little deeper into how you can accomplish this.

When making a promise, be clear about what you're committing to. Clearly articulate all expectations, specifics about deliverables, and any relevant deadlines or conditions. Ensure that both parties have a shared understanding of what is being promised. Once you've made a promise, it's crucial that you honor it. Treat your commitments as priorities and follow through on them diligently. Strive to deliver what you promised within the agreed-upon time frame and to the best of your abilities. To achieve this, break down your commitments into manageable tasks, create a timeline, and allocate resources accordingly. Stay organized and remain on top of the individual commitments that make up your promise, in order to avoid delays or oversights.

Another challenge is the inevitability of surprises. When this happens, it's important to handle surprises in ways that build respect. Should any unforeseen circumstances arise that prevent you from fulfilling a promise, communicate that fact with the involved parties as soon as possible. Be honest and transparent about the situation, explain the reasons for the delay or inability to deliver, and propose alternative solutions or a revised timeline. If you encounter difficulties in fulfilling a promise, take ownership of the problem. Admit your error, apologize if necessary, and work toward rectifying the situation. Taking responsibility demonstrates that you have integrity and are committed to making things right.

Based on your analysis of what happened, develop strategies and action steps to prevent similar mistakes from occurring in the future. Adjust your decision-making practice, behaviors, or processes in order to incorporate the lessons you've learned. Implement changes that will lead to better outcomes or mitigate the risk of repeating the same errors.

It is worth noting that learning from mistakes doesn't mean that you have to avoid risks altogether. Learning involves taking calculated risks and being open to the possibility of making new mistakes. Use the knowledge you gained from past errors to make better-informed decisions and to navigate future challenges more effectively. The true value of learning from mistakes lies in applying the lessons to your future actions. Put your newfound knowledge into practice, and actively integrate it into your decision-making and behaviors.

To improve your ability to deliver on your commitments, consider implementing systems or practices that help you stay accountable. This could include setting reminders, using task management tools, seeking support or feedback from others, and establishing regular check-ins to assess progress.

Make a practice of reflecting regularly on your actions, decisions, and experiences, and learn from your successes and failures so that you can refine and strengthen your integrity. Continuously pursue personal growth and self-improvement. Remember, integrity is not about perfection but about consistently striving to align your actions with your values and principles. When you cultivate integrity, you build a strong personal foundation, foster trust with others, and contribute to a more ethical and principled society. By examining your commitments and ensuring they align with your values, you can maintain a strong sense of integrity and achieve greater personal and professional fulfillment.

Conclusion: Leadership with Integrity

At its heart, leading with integrity is a function of being a reliable leader. Such leaders honor their word and are honest about the promises they make to themselves and others. When leaders exhibit reliable behavior, positive results follow. Such leaders are true to themselves, and their promises show them to be trustworthy and dependable. Trust is at the foundation of all successful long-serving organizations and leaders.

Purpose

A MISSILE STRIKE ON POLAND

In our constantly changing world, in which uncertainties loom over every horizon, it is important for individuals, especially leaders, to find their purpose. Reflecting on this, I remember November 15, 2022, when a missile struck the Polish village of Przewodów, near the border of Ukraine. This fateful day served as a stark reminder of the fragility of peace.

Not suspecting the chaos that was about to unfold that morning, I followed my usual morning routine. I woke up early, embraced the stillness of dawn, and engaged in my morning prayers. With a sense of peace, I made myself a warm bowl of oatmeal, eagerly anticipating the moment when I would add raisins to enhance its flavor. As I prepared to enjoy my breakfast, I absentmindedly scrolled through social media, seeking a simple moment of distraction.

However, the news that awaited me was far from ordinary. My eyes widened in disbelief as I read about the missile strike. The initial thought that rushed through my mind was one of sheer terror: Could this be the beginning of World War III?

The strike had hit Poland, sparking concerns that this act of aggression might have been a deliberate attack by Russia on a NATO member. As the news spread like wildfire, fear and uncertainty gripped the hearts of people worldwide. Diplomatic efforts intensified, with shuttle diplomacy—which *Oxford Reference* defines as "negotiations conducted by a mediator who travels between two or more parties that are reluctant to hold direct discussions"—taking center stage as multiple nations sought to swiftly address the situation. The twenty-four seven news coverage served as a constant reminder that the world was teetering on the edge of turmoil, with peace hanging by a thread.

Amid this chaos, people began to question the meaning and purpose of their lives. To me, this swift escalation of events highlighted the importance of finding a personal mission that transcends volatile circumstances. It had become evident that in this ever-changing world, having a sense of purpose is essential to navigating the stormy seas of uncertainty.

In such times of crisis, some people turn to their faith, seeking solace and guidance. Others engage in introspection, examining their passions and values, determined to make a positive impact in a world in flux. However you respond, you may realize that by understanding your purpose and aligning your actions with it, you can contribute to the shaping of a better future.

As people's anxieties and speculations regarding the missile strike in Poland were spiking, the investigation into the incident began. Hours turned into days before it was eventually determined that it had not been an intentional Russian attack on Poland. Although the danger of a larger conflict subsided, the echoes of that event continued to reverberate, leaving a lasting impact on those who experienced it. The world did not return to its previous state of equilibrium. Instead, it continued to evolve and change, as it always has and as it always will. Some people understand that their sense of purpose is a guiding force; these are the ones who are prepared to face the ever-shifting world with renewed determination and resilience.

The missile strike, among other lessons, cemented for me the knowledge that life can transform in an instant, and that no one can predict what lies ahead. If it is true that we are always facing uncertainty—and it is—then knowing our purpose is even more significant.

When we recognize our passions, values, and aspirations, we get empowered to navigate the constantly changing world with purpose, and to create a meaningful impact in our lives and the lives of others. I knew this already when the missile hit Przewodów. You see, earlier that year, I had had to navigate another change in my life.

In the brisk winter of mid-January 2022, I'd found myself embarking on a new chapter of my life as I moved to Washington, DC, as my family stayed in our home state and later traveled to East Africa. My emotions swirled within me as I settled into my new apartment, a mere stone's throw away from the epicenter of global power.

Washington, DC, is a city pulsating with energy, where decisions that shape the world are made. For me, it was also the place where my dreams of influencing foreign policy had the potential to become reality. Excitement filled the air as I prepared for my first official event at the prestigious State Department. The anticipation of what lay ahead was palpable, and I couldn't help but feel a sense of awe. The hallowed halls of diplomacy beckoned, and I was ready to embrace the challenges and opportunities that awaited me.

I had already determined that leading is my purpose in life, including guiding other leaders as they embrace their potential to create exponential impact for the prosperity of organizations and society. In DC, I found that I was able to explore my values further with trusted partners and professionals. I was able to develop and reflect on my core values, such as supporting purpose-driven leaders who want to achieve a higher impact by embracing transformational leadership models—models that in turn translate intangible challenges into tangible results, creating shared value and prosperity for organizations, and for the world.

I can say all that boldly now, but one of the challenges I faced early in my career was articulating my purpose and values clearly. If you cannot articulate your purpose, this will have huge implications on your ability to develop authentic, trusted relationships. Admittedly, doing so is not an easy undertaking. It takes a long time to reflect, clarify your purpose, and discuss it with trusted partners, but it is well worth the effort. Once I was able to identify my purpose and values, my leadership—both professionally and personally—was completely transformed.

On the day of the State Department event, a surge of nerves mixed with anticipation coursed through my veins. I dressed in my finest gray suit, much like one my father used to wear (except mine is slim fit), ensuring that I presented myself with confidence and with a professionalism befitting the occasion. My job centered on the strengthening of democracy, an important theme that resonates deeply with me.

I remember walking into the State Department building and marveling at its grandeur and historical significance. The weight of the world seemed to rest on its imposing pillars, reminding me of the responsibility and privilege that come with being a part of this institution. Here, ideas collide and nations converse. Here, global relationships are forged.

That first day, I was welcomed by Under Secretary Uzra Zeya, my old friend and new boss. Together, we joined Secretary of State Tony Blinken and others at a ceremony for the State Department's cafeteria, which was being renamed after Ambassador Terence Todman: a pioneering African American diplomat who served as ambassador to six countries. It was a loaded and promising start.

In the following days, I would hear speeches that stirred hearts. I would explore historical struggles and triumphs related to the goal of achieving inclusion in foreign policy. I would interact with the stories of pioneers who fought tirelessly for equality and representation. I would find myself engrossed in discussions and dialogues surrounding the theme of inclusion. Prominent figures in the field would share their experiences with me, shedding light on the challenges they faced and the progress they had made. Listening to others is always a humbling and enlightening experience, one that reminds me of the immense power that lies in diversity and understanding.

My decision to move to Washington, DC, proved to be the catalyst for transformative experiences. It was in this vibrant city, brimming with ambition and power, that I discovered, connected with, and explored my purpose with people I grew to trust. It was here that, through my work of influencing foreign policy, I learned that true power lies not only in the corridors of institutions but also in the hearts and minds of those who dare to dream of a better world: one that's driven by purpose. In this place, I truly started to live my purpose.

THE INSPIRATION OF R. T. RYBAK

How did I know my purpose? Its discovery began with inspiration. Anything can inspire a person. Faith, family, culture, and childhood experiences all can inform purpose. The lessons gained from education, work, and fun times can reveal purpose. I personally find my purpose when an idea moves or inspires me. Knowing my purpose is an ongoing process. I continue to learn from new insights and be inspired by new people.

One helpful way to explore purpose is through conversations, especially conversations with a teacher, a mentor, or a friend. Connecting on a deep level helps me consider new perspectives and forge meaningful relationships, and it helps me understand myself better. Ongoing conversations with my friend and mentor R. T. Rybak, for example, play an important role in helping me stay present and connected with my purpose.

R. T. Rybak is a distinguished leader who serves as the CEO of the Minneapolis Foundation and previously served as the mayor of Minneapolis. R. T. is also a prominent advocate for civic engagement. I first met R. T. in 2010 at a community-organized vigil. Two cousins of mine, Osman and Mohamed, had been murdered during a robbery at the Seward Market and Halal Meat in Minneapolis, and I'd traveled from San Diego to support my family. I was impressed by how the city's mayor showed up for the victims' families and for the city's new immigrant communities.

Later, when I moved with my wife and children to Minneapolis in 2012, Rybak was among the few leaders in this new city whom I knew. I reached out to Rybak and he became a mentor. Through our conversations, it became clear that he knew a lot about democracy, and I was happy to tap into this knowledge. Rybak listened to my impassioned words as I advocated for the inclusion of racial, ethnic, and religious minority groups in building healthy democracies in the U.S. and beyond. As I talked with Rybak, I was inspired by his stories: about his two terms in office as mayor; his experience as a vice chair of the Democratic National Committee; his decision to become the first mayor of a major city in the U.S. to endorse President Barack Obama's 2008 campaign; and his later choice to lead a civic institution, the Minneapolis Foundation.

Responding to my passions, Rybak introduced me to public- and private-sector leaders, and when I decided to launch Tayo Consulting Group—a social enterprise offering a new model for partnerships between business, philanthropy, non-governmental organizations (NGOs), and local government—Rybak provided me support. He helped me identify and articulate my purpose as a transformational leader who promotes and works to strengthen democracy and an equitable economy for all.

MY PURPOSE: EQUITABLE ECONOMY AND INCLUSIVE DEMOCRACY

Through these conversations, I discovered my conviction that I needed to share my knowledge, expertise, and connections with others, and to help advance important policy priorities designed to welcome refugees and address today's workforce needs in a way that honors the dignity of all stakeholders. This work deeply hinged on my values.

I believe, for example, in ensuring that more refugee and immigrant leaders, and immigrant-led organizations, have strong links to established organizations that are working on issues related to education, health, and economic empowerment. My encouragement of refugee leaders to take risks to work together and increase their power through transformational leadership is driven by my values. Inviting business and philanthropic partners to get a little uncomfortable by supporting partnership models that are new to them is another way I demonstrate my values through action.

I doubt I would be working in the State Department today if I wasn't committed to living in my purpose and to constantly living out my values. Even the work I do to address the economic and democratic needs of our society today is fueled by my values. For me, this work has been more than just a professional pursuit; it has been a manifestation of my core values, which guide me as I take action and work to make a lasting impact. From the very beginning of my career journey, I have recognized the importance of economic prosperity to individual success and understood that a strong and inclusive economy lays the foundation for a thriving society. It was with this conviction that I set out on my path to contribute to the economic well-being of people.

I have always sought ways to create opportunities for people and communities to prosper, a motivation that led me to cofound a social enterprise called BanQu, which I will discuss in more detail later in the book. Whether I've been promoting entrepreneurship, supporting small businesses, or advocating for equitable economic policies, I have always felt the conviction to uplift those who are underinvested in financially and empower them to achieve their fullest potential. Because I recognize the interconnectedness of economic success and social progress, I aim to foster a society in which everyone has a fair chance to thrive.

In parallel with these beliefs, I came to recognize that a robust democracy is indispensable for safeguarding our collective values and ensuring that the voices of the people are heard. That is how democracy-strengthening became an essential part of my journey, driven by my unwavering belief in the power of participatory governance.

Over time, I have actively engaged in initiatives that aim to enhance democratic institutions, promote transparency, and increase civic engagement. By encouraging people to actively participate in shaping their communities, and by advocating for policies that promote social justice and equal representation, I hope to fortify the very foundation on which our society thrives.

As you can see, the role of trusted partners has been instrumental to me throughout this journey. Long ago, I recognized that I couldn't affect meaningful change alone. That is why, even in this seemingly personal endeavor of articulating and living out my purpose, I have talked with like-minded people like R. T. Rybak, as well as many others whom I have not mentioned in this chapter, but who also share my values and vision. Together, we have forged alliances, pooled resources, and harnessed collective wisdom to amplify our impact.

These trusted partnerships have also helped with the work of soul-searching. Through open dialogue and a commitment to shared goals, we have been able to navigate conflicting values and find answers to difficult internal questions. By continuing to reflect on my values and by exploring new avenues with my trusted partners, I have ensured that my efforts remain relevant and responsive to the evolving needs of our society.

I can say without batting an eye that it is through this alignment of values, these actions, and my collaboration with others that I have found success. But success, to me, is not measured solely by personal achievements. It is measured by the positive and lasting impact I am able to make in the lives of others and in the broader society.

With this in mind, I remain steadfast in my commitment to addressing the economic needs, and the need for democracy-strengthening, within our society. I remain committed to the value of transformational leadership. I constantly seek ways to refine my approach, adapt to new challenges, and embrace emerging opportunities. I know always that by staying true to my values and embracing the power of collaboration, I can contribute to building a society that is prosperous, just, and inclusive for all.

UZRA ZEYA: FROM SHARED PURPOSE TO SHARED WORK

Conversations about values do more than center a leader's values; they also build deep relationships between leaders, and where there are shared values, it can be easier to do shared work. An example of this is my relationship with Uzra Zeya, a diplomat with over three decades of experience in U.S. foreign policy work. In 2019, she took on the position of CEO and president at the Alliance for Peacebuilding, having left the Trump administration the year before after calling out the administration's practices of excluding minorities from top leadership positions in the State Department and embassies abroad. That year, when we first met, our planned one-hour conversation easily extended to more than two hours as we discovered the many things we had in common.

A child of immigrants from India, she shared my willingness to push against the status quo. In a lot of ways, we had experienced parallel journeys. We both had a global consciousness as well, and were committed to the pursuit of localized solutions. Uzra said to me, "You've got to allow countries to reflect their traditions, their histories, their modes of consensus building, and not imagine that it's going to be a mirror image of what we have in the United States." Through our conversations, I learned how she was living out her purpose, and she helped me to explore and understand my purpose too.

Uzra believes strongly that strengthening democracy in the United States is essential to encouraging and strengthening democracy around the world, and so do I. She shared with me her opinion, "Freedom of association allows a vibrant, robust civil society that includes young people holding the government accountable. When civil society thrives, it drives change for a truly just, inclusive, and peaceful world."

Uzra was pleased to learn about the multitude of civil-society partnerships that I had formed across sectors: business, nonprofit, education, peacebuilding, healthcare, philanthropy, and social entrepreneurship. She believes that it is only through cross-sector partnerships that democracy can be promoted at home and abroad.

After a while, she asked me to serve as a volunteer senior fellow with Alliance for Peacebuilding, providing advisory services to her and her leadership team. In this role, I offered my insights regarding a cross-sector approach to advancing human dignity through peacebuilding. As a result of this work, Alliance for Peacebuilding awarded me the Melanie Greenberg Award of Excellence at PeaceCon 2019. This prestigious award was named after the organization's former CEO: a courageous peacebuilder and a longtime friend of mine. The following year, Uzra invited me to speak at a public conversation on U.S. polarization. There, I discussed what peacebuilders can learn from U.S. and international civil-society partners. More importantly, I got to live out my purpose through each one of my interactions with her.

After the election of President Joe Biden, Uzra and I both applied for, and were appointed to, roles in the Biden administration. When

I wrestled with the question of whether coming to DC was true to my purpose, I took comfort in knowing that I would be working with and for Under Secretary Uzra Zeya. Through our conversations, each of us had heard how the other lived out the values we share.

EXPLORE YOUR VALUES WITH TRUSTED PARTNERS

Knowing your purpose and values makes it possible for you to choose a community that allows you to exemplify them and multiply their impact. By purpose, I mean your reason for existing or for engaging in an activity.

Finding purpose entails developing a clear understanding of your goals and values, which give direction and meaning to your life. I know for a fact that developing this sense of purpose is important for personal and professional growth, as it provides a framework for making and evaluating decisions, and it also helps people set priorities. Finding your purpose also creates satisfaction in life and gives you the resilience you need to overcome obstacles and setbacks.

When attempting to figure out what your purpose is, you might think about something and wonder, *Is this something I value?* Following is a brief test for core values created by Ronnie Brooks, the founding director of the James P. Shannon Leadership Institute, which can help you.

A cross-sector leader herself, Brooks not only forms leaders, she also provides leadership herself within both the government and nonprofits. I have used this test to confirm my own foundational values. According to Brooks, "The test of a true core value [is that] you would do it despite consequences. You choose it freely, from genuine alternatives. You act on it all the time. It applies everywhere in your work. It lasts over time. It gives you pride."

The work of finding and defining your purpose can be a lifelong journey, one that involves exploring your values, interests, and strengths. It may also involve taking risks and stepping outside of your comfort zone in order to pursue new opportunities and experiences. While the process of discovering your purpose can be challenging, it can ultimately lead to a more fulfilling life.

Here are some steps you can take to define and articulate your purpose:

1. Identify and reflect on your values.

Reflect on your core values and principles. Consider what matters most to you, and think about the ethical standards you want to uphold. Clarify your personal beliefs and the qualities you want to embody in your actions and decisions, and be honest with yourself as you engage in this exercise. Think about your choices, actions, and behavior. Do they align? Are there areas where you fall short of your values? How can you improve?

Your values reflect what you cherish and play a significant role in shaping and influencing your sense of purpose. They also provide a strong foundation for pursuing meaningful goals and actions. They influence your decision-making and help you make choices that align with your purpose. For example, when faced with a moral dilemma, your values will act as a compass and guide you toward choices that align with your core beliefs. Will you give a bribe to get a service faster or would you rather take the official channels? Knowing what you value can guide you toward making the best decision.

Values also provide a framework for evaluating opportunities, assessing trade-offs, and prioritizing actions. Have you ever turned down a lucrative job offer in favor of a different opportunity where your work could make a difference for the world? If so, this means your value system is at work, and it made you prioritize the needs of others at the expense of earning a greater income.

When your sense of purpose is supported by your values, it contributes to long-term satisfaction and fulfillment. Pursuing goals and actions that are in harmony with your values leads to a sense of coherence and fulfillment. Living in alignment with your values and purpose creates a sense of well-being, as you feel true to yourself and live according to what truly matters to you.

2. Clarify your standards and identify your passions.

Based on your values, identify clear ethical standards and define the kind of actions and behaviors that align with them. Working with Uzra Zeya and R. T. Rybak helped me with this. For example, each project that I undertook had to tie back to my passion. I remember the countless hours I spent with my trusted partners, working to understand the reasons behind the choices I made. The goal is to always choose projects that also support your passions and are consistent with your personal standards.

Acting in this way gives you a clear framework to guide you whenever you need to make a decision. Ensure that you believe in the standards you've set, and keep yourself accountable. The idea is to have your actions guided by these standards, to learn from the times you fall short, and to commit to making changes when they are needed.

When I talk about passions, I'm referring to the things that excite and motivate you, such as a hobby or a cause you care deeply about. If you have a strong passion for leadership, it will lead you on a journey of self-discovery and personal development. This passion will provide the initial spark that ignites your curiosity and drive your motivation to take action, such as enrolling in a leadership training program. It will also propel you to seek out opportunities where you can exercise your leadership abilities and grow. When you are passionate about something, you are more likely to invest time, energy, and effort into it, even when faced with obstacles or challenges. This passion to succeed will give you the drive to overcome setbacks, persist through difficulties, and stay focused on your long-term goals.

3. Seek wisdom.

Seek out wisdom through conversations with mentors, as I've described doing. Also take in the words of authors and remember what your mentors have taught you in the past. Seek wisdom from books, speakers, and spiritual traditions wherever you can. They are treasure troves of knowledge and insight that can be used to shape perspectives and guide actions. They remind the rest of us that the quest for knowledge and self-improvement is an ongoing, enriching journey and that the wisdom gained from these sources can illuminate our path toward greater understanding and fulfillment.

For example, these words of Oprah Winfrey are an inspiration to me: "The biggest adventure you can ever take is to live the life of your dreams. Be prepared—when you finally summon the courage to cast a vote for yourself, you can expect obstacles. The whole world will rise up to tell you who you cannot become and what you cannot do." But Winfrey challenges people to be centered on two questions, "Who am I? And what do I want?"

Conclusion: Purposeful Leadership

At its most basic level, purposeful leadership in an individual involves identifying the unique values that person has that are fundamental to being a leader. Achieving this self-awareness is an ongoing process that is aided by engaging conversations with people who inspire the person. When leaders exhibit such behavior, they enjoy a meaningful life. The outcome of this self-reflection is the development of a necessary framework that organizations and individuals can use to make decisions, overcome obstacles, and impact the world.

Accountability

THE U.S. PRESIDENTIAL ELECTION OF 2016

Some people today, the former president elected in November 2016 among them, say that refugees don't belong in the United States. During his first presidential campaign, then-candidate Donald Trump called the migration of Muslims, including children, a Trojan Horse, suggesting that these refugees could be a source of destruction and terror. Two days before the 2016 election, he came to Minnesota, where he spoke out against Somali refugees specifically. At a campaign rally held in Minneapolis, he said that the state has "suffered enough" from refugees and spoke of banning refugee resettlement in the U.S.

Once elected, leaders are accountable to voters for their promises, and the 2016 elections in the United States were highly consequential and marked by intense political tensions and polarization. It was a presidential election that captivated the nation and had far-reaching implications for the future of American politics. The race

49

for the presidency primarily revolved around two major party candidates: Hillary Clinton, representing the Democratic Party, and Donald Trump, representing the Republican Party. Both candidates had distinct backgrounds, policies, and visions for the country, leading to a deeply divided electorate.

The election campaign was characterized by fierce debates, heated rhetoric, and extensive media coverage. Issues such as immigration, national security, the economy, healthcare, and social matters took center stage, fueling passionate discussions across the nation. The election cycle was notable for the unconventional campaign style of Donald Trump. His messages resonated with many who felt disillusioned with the political establishment, as he positioned himself as an outsider seeking to disrupt the status quo. Trump's promises regarding economic revitalization and securing the U.S.'s southern border, and his campaign slogan, "Make America great again," resonated with a significant portion of the electorate.

By contrast, Hillary Clinton, a former Secretary of State and First Lady, emphasized her experience, qualifications, and commitment to progressive policies. She shared her vision of building upon the legacy of the Obama administration and advancing issues such as healthcare reform, gun control, and social justice. She was my candidate of choice.

As Election Day approached, tensions ran high, and both campaigns intensified their efforts to mobilize supporters. The outcome of the election hinged on key swing states, where both candidates invested significant resources and held numerous rallies to secure crucial votes.

During that period, I was busy laying the foundation for the new company I had cofounded, BanQu. However, I still took time to lead and organize with a coalition of Somali American leaders in my community to increase voter turnout.

Ultimately, to the surprise of many pollsters and political pundits, Donald Trump emerged victorious, winning the Electoral College and securing the presidency. Though he had lost the popular vote, his electoral success reflected deep divisions within American society and a growing sense of frustration with the political establishment. Within immigrant communities, Muslim communities, and communities of color, there was less surprise that Americans would elect a president who expressed racist, Islamophobic, and xenophobic ideas. These communities feared that the new president, accountable to voters who'd responded to his rhetoric, would continue to make people like us out to be the enemy.

"DO WE HAVE TO MOVE AGAIN?"

As the election results settled in during the following days, they cast a shadow of doubt and apprehension over my family. At one point, my eldest daughter, Samia, turned to me and asked me a question that seemed to be weighing heavily on her mind.

"Do we have to move again?" she asked, her voice laced with worry and uncertainty.

The question struck a chord deep within my heart, as I was aware of the fear that lay behind it. I had asked my father the same question when I was a boy in Mogadishu.

With an unwavering resolve, I looked into my daughter's eyes and replied, "No, my love. You belong here, and I will do everything I can to make sure you continue to belong here." I hope she picked up on my conviction as I spoke those words. I hope they gave her confidence and allayed her fears.

In that moment, I made a promise. I committed to shielding my children from the turbulence that threatens to uproot their sense of belonging in this country. I understand the importance of stability and security in their lives, and I resolved that I would spare no effort to ensure it. Like my father before me, I am responsible for my children and accountable to my children. I hope I am a pillar of strength my family can count on. Along with my wife, I make the effort to know our neighbors, to attend community events, and to foster inclusivity, understanding, and unity. These choices are a testament to my unwavering determination to create a nurturing environment for my children.

War displaced their great-grandmother and their great-grandfather. It displaced their grandmother, their grandfather, and their mother. The war displaced me. Every day, I wonder: What can I do to make sure that the same fate does not befall them? I keep my children very, very close to my heart. Perhaps that's because when I was a child very close to their current ages, I had to take up unexpected responsibilities.

When I was a boy, I had a bedroom, a classroom full of friends, and a beach nearby. Mogadishu was my whole life. Then one day war broke out in Somalia, and that all changed. My parents, my siblings, and I had to flee to a camp in another country. That's when I became a refugee. I had never heard that word before. The camp gave me a number. I was no longer Hamse Warfa. I was simply a boy who couldn't go back home. I didn't know where my life would go next.

After the 2016 election, that feeling returned to me. Once again, I didn't know where my family's lives would go. Still, I made a promise to my children. I knew it was my mission to be useful to society by ensuring that my children belong in this country.

The sweetness and innocence of my children have kept me focused on my mission. As a father, I have responsibilities in raising them. Their mother and I feed them, we house them, we teach them, and we love them. I pray that I will always stay accountable when it comes to these responsibilities.

AN AMERICAN IN AFRICA OR AN AFRICAN IN AMERICA?

At BanQu, the start-up technology business I cofounded, I had the responsibility of helping refugees around the world find a home after they'd lost the only home they knew. In this role, just after the election, I left for Kenya. I wasn't sure how much longer I would be able to go there freely. I needed to listen to the needs of refugees directly. Only then would I be able to figure out how to align the needs of these refugees with the needs of my country and my children.

While I was in Kenya in January 2017, President Donald Trump issued his first Muslim travel ban. I was set to return to the United States on January 28. The executive order banned visitors, immigrants, and refugees from Somalia and six other Muslim countries from entering the U.S. I felt trapped between two places. Was I an American in Africa, or an African in America?

I arrived early at the airport in Kenya. I was emotional. As a citizen of the United States, I was allowed to travel, but the policy still felt personal to me. If the travel ban had been in place in the 1990s, I could never have come to the United States as a refugee.

The airport was chaotic. There, I met dozens of Somali Minnesotans who held green cards but were not yet citizens. Three of these worried travelers were friends of mine. They were in Kenya on business, like me, and caring for family.

One mother in tears cried out, afraid that she would not see her children again. I comforted her. These travelers had many questions, and it pained me that I did not have clear answers. Many asked to stay with me throughout the journey, hoping my status as a U.S. citizen might help me to get them answers or to advocate for them.

Even as I was comforting these travelers, I felt stuck. I was powerless to help these victims of President Trump. I was sad, angry, and frustrated, but I tried to act calmly.

Friends from around the world reached out to me. Knowing I was in

Kenya, they checked in about my situation and safety. I asked my friends to pray for me and my fellow travelers. I shared my flight information so that friends could await my return. I connected to lawyers who were willing to meet the plane in Minneapolis. I took strength from the prayers being offered up by others.

Finally, I landed in Minnesota. Wow, I felt so good! My return, however, was not an answer to the problems of the travel ban. As a result of the Trump administration's policies, over seventy-nine thousand Muslims with visas to travel to the United States were rejected. The impact of this first travel ban was immediate. I vowed to work even harder to create solutions for the families who remained in the refugee camps.

This United States has a dark side. In the course of its early history, indigenous people were forced from their homes and almost erased by white settlers. Following my trip to Kenya, I traveled to the Minnesota History Center to better learn what those same white settlers did to fellow European immigrants who came to the U.S. after them. While I was there, I realized that all-American-sounding names such as Andersen and Kennedy had once been as foreign in this land as the name Hamse Warfa.

As I flipped through the documents, I read about a department of the Minnesota government that existed during World War I. It was called the Minnesota Commission of Public Safety. Its legal purpose had been to build support for the war effort. But its leaders and agents became too powerful. They ended up attacking specific cultures of European immigrants who'd fled Europe and never wanted to fight in its wars again.

I'll never forget reading a letter one commission leader, one Judge John F. McGee, sent to one of Minnesota's senators, which read in part: "If the Governor appoints men who have backbone . . . the street corner orators who . . . denounce the army, and advise against enlistments, will be looking through the barbed fences of an internment camp out on the prairie somewhere."

Reading that, it hit me that the refugee story is an old story. At the time that John McGee wrote his letter, immigrants who came to this country searching for opportunities were told to abandon their language, their food, and their memories of home, but many of them held on just like we do. Our cultural differences are not something that should be changed by the government but rather something to be celebrated and shared and adapted, a way to meet new challenges offered by free people who believe diversity is a benefit, not a deficit.

STAY ACCOUNTABLE

Accountability demands honesty. It is about results and outcomes. While integrity can exist inside a person, accountability is experienced in the world. I am confident that my children's generation will, while drawing from their traditions, continue to come up with new ways for everyone in this world to live in peace and prosperity, and to feel valued and respected. I am confident that they will know that they are not alone. I know that they will help each other keep mercy in their hearts, believing that they belong here. I know this because of the work our communities have done, the stories we have told, and how accountable we have stayed.

When I talk about accountability, I am referring to the work of taking responsibility for one's circumstances and mistakes, communicating clearly and honestly with others about them, following through on one's commitments, and being willing to learn from other people's feedback. Accountability entails setting clear standards of personal conduct and being willing to hold oneself and others to those standards.

It was accountability that kept me from simply complaining and wallowing in 2016 when Donald Trump's speech turned refugees into enemies. It was accountability that fueled my work on behalf of my children and of refugees like me. It was accountability that would later prompt me to work with Minnesota governor Tim Walz's office to help rebuild small businesses following the civil unrest that was triggered by the murder of George Floyd. It is accountability that has kept me in every role that I have taken up throughout my career. Being accountable entails making commitments that you can keep and being transparent with your intentions and decisions.

BE KNOWN BY THE POWER OF YOUR WORD

Accountability is the outcome of purposeful commitments made in relationships of integrity. Accountability can be personal in nature, as demonstrated by the example of my commitment to my children following the election of Donald Trump. It can also be public and political, as in the case of the 2016 presidential election and the resulting Muslim travel ban. As my visit to the Minnesota Historical Society demonstrated, accountability can also unfold over generations. The commitments of the past reverberate in today's world, for good and for bad.

If you want to be powerful, and if you want to be known as a leader, you need to be accountable. Your actions must reflect the words that you use. Your words and your actions are how people get to know you. When people see that they can rely on you, they will trust you with greater responsibility. Now, being accountable does not necessarily mean that you are good. As the example of the Muslim travel ban demonstrates, being powerful can result in hurtful policy and ugly leadership. Still, you can't be a good leader without accountability.

Here are some steps you can take to become a consistently accountable leader:

1. **Be intentional with your commitments.**

Accountability demands that, in the course of making a decision, you review your values, goals, and resources to ensure that they can support the fulfillment of any commitment you are about to make. This is about weighing your circumstances to determine what opportunities to say yes to and which ones to decline. Let me tell you a short story about accountability.

Alice, a Washington-based psychologist, told me that after analyzing her database of contacts over one year, she realized that about 60 percent of all her non-business phone calls that she'd received during that time were from people asking her to do things for them. This included friends and relatives who wanted to borrow cash from her, a neighbor requesting that she pick up the neighbor's kids from school on her way home from work, invitations to attend community fundraisers, and more.

"I realized that I would need to have superhuman powers to meet all societal demands on my time and resources. To remain sane and focused on my goals, I had to learn to say no to most such requests," she said. "I thought that people would dislike me for not being there for them, but I later realized that they respected me more for being principled, and for being there for the few requests that I accepted."

From Alice, I learned the importance of first taking into account whether the requests being made on my time and resources align with my goals and values. I now review each one to see if it is feasible given my available time and resources, and I weigh whether agreeing will contribute to a win-win outcome for me and the person making the request. This is the essence of accountability.

I also learned that being intentional means honoring the commitments you have already made. This requires taking responsibility for your choices and following through on your obligations, even when doing so becomes challenging or inconvenient. Being intentional involves continually evaluating your commitments and assessing whether they still align with your values and goals. Doing this will help you see which commitments no longer align with your purpose and free you to let them go.

Of course, you will need to communicate clearly to avoid making commitments that may seem ambiguous or creating expectations you might not be able to fulfill. When you say yes, your answer must be clear, with any limits to your commitment clearly articulated. For example, if a friend requests that you join him for a lunchtime meeting, you might need to explain that you will only be available for an hour, between 1:00 and 2:00 p.m., at which point you will have to be excused to attend to other matters of the day. After you've established this, when you attend the meeting, be sure to leave at the time that you stated you would leave.

Ultimately, being intentional with your commitments requires self-awareness, reflection, and a willingness to make choices that align with your values and goals. Acting in this way can lead you to a more purposeful and fulfilling life. Being accountable brings your integrity and your purpose together to help you create outcomes that the world needs.

2. Be honest and transparent.

Honesty and transparency are two fundamental aspects of building trust, maintaining healthy relationships, and fostering effective communication. Being a good leader involves being truthful, open, and authentic in your interactions with others.

To be clear, being honest and transparent doesn't mean indiscriminately revealing everything about yourself or others. As a leader, you are entitled to your private life, and on the professional front, some of the details about the programs you are working on might need to be disclosed to the people you're dealing with only at the right time. There will be boundaries of confidentiality and privacy that need to be observed, so you will need to be discerning about what information is appropriate to share in different contexts.

Having given the disclaimer above, I must also emphasize that being honest means telling the truth and representing things as they are, to the best of your knowledge. Some truths are difficult to share, but speaking the uncomfortable truth could be the right thing to do.

When you make a mistake or realize you were wrong, be willing to admit it. This is what transformational leaders do. Taking responsibility for your actions shows integrity and demonstrates that you value honesty and accountability. By practicing honesty and transparency, you build stronger connections, establish trust, and create an environment that's conducive to growth and collaboration.

3. Set meaningful goals.

Setting meaningful goals that align with your purpose brings fulfillment in life. Goal setting commonly begins with the crucial step of taking the time to reflect on your purpose. Doing this helps you to gain clarity about what truly matters to you. Consider your values, passions, and the impact you want to make in the world. Ask yourself questions like: What do I care deeply about? What brings me joy and fulfillment? How do I want to contribute to others or a cause?

Identify the key areas of your life that are most closely connected to your purpose—such as your career, personal growth, relationships, health and well-being, and community involvement—and use them to sharpen your focus and attention.

There is a popular framework that you can use to help you set goals within each of these areas. This framework builds from the idea that goals can be divided into two parts: objectives and key results (popularly known as OKR).

Under the OKR model, objectives answer the question of *what* you want to do and describe the place you hope to be, while the key results answer the *how*, providing a roadmap for getting to the what. An objective describes a goal and puts a deadline to it, while key results give you benchmarks for measuring progress toward that objective. Generally, you can have between three and five key results for one objective.

OKRs establish a mindset that can help you get where you want to be with confidence. This often involves moving from general to more specific thinking. Look at it this way: Knowing that you want to "end poverty," for example, or "inspire leaders" is not enough. What will you do next to try to reach those goals? That's the question OKRs help you to answer. They define your highest priorities for the next month or quarter. They ask you for extraordinary performance.

As you write down your OKRs, make sure your objectives connect to your greater mission. Are they meaningful enough to point you in a clear direction? Are they audacious enough to bring about significant change when they are achieved? Are they inspiring? If the answer is yes, then the objectives you've set are effective ones. While at it, test your key results for effectiveness by making sure the answer to the following three questions is yes: Are they timebound and specific? Are they aggressive and realistic? Are they verifiable and measurable?

While I was working at the State of Minnesota as deputy commissioner for the Department of Employment and Economic Development (DEED), my team used the OKR framework for our goal setting. We realized that if we were going to lead post-pandemic economic recovery in Minnesota, we needed to be able to set good goals and measure results well. When we began in 2019, we had five objectives, one of which was building a positive internal culture within the organization. For that objective, we identified several key results: reducing regrettable attrition numbers by 25 percent, turning our net promoter score positive, and ensuring that all our employees were given clear performance indicators and received a performance review every year.

Consider using the following set of metrics to grade your outcomes. Grading OKRs gives you an opportunity to reflect on accomplishments and figure out what you could have done differently. Use a 0.0 to 1.0 grading scale so that when you have performed well, the key result scores fall between 0.6 and 0.7. When I was working for the State of Minnesota, all of our OKRs scored within that range.

As a rule, when you are nearing the end of each OKR, score it by determining whether you were able to meet your key results. As an alternative to the 0 to 1 grading scale, you might use the traffic light system, in which red represents areas where you did not make progress, yellow represents goals where you made progress but did not reach completion, and green represents objectives that were delivered.

Reassess those objectives that have low scores. High scores are proof that you are working in the right direction. It is possible to purchase OKR software that will score the key results for you automatically, but you can also do it for yourself.

Remember, setting meaningful goals is an ongoing process. As you gain new insights, refine your purpose, or experience shifts in your life, your goals may evolve. Continually aligning your goals with your purpose will ensure that you are continuously progressing toward a life that is meaningful, fulfilling, and in harmony with your deepest values and aspirations.

4.   Ask to be held responsible for your goals.

Share your goals with one or more trusted individuals who can provide support and hold you accountable. This could include a mentor, coach, friend, or family member. Regularly discuss your progress, challenges, and insights with them, as their perspective and encouragement can be valuable in helping you stay focused on your purpose-driven goals. It can be hard to trust people, but great change does not happen in isolation, and learning how to include trusted partners in the small things will help you build trust with others when you are working on bigger things.

The people you ask to hold you accountable may include not just long trusted partners but also new friends, colleagues, and even strangers. You may not want to do this right away, as you want to first show success to new partners. But as you progress in your goals, it is important to introduce yourself to others in relationship to your goals. We become known by who we say we are, and by what we say our goals are. In fact, sometimes when we adopt new goals, strangers are the most likely to believe us because they don't know us in other ways. When you are accountable, you are known by your word. People know who you are because that's who you say you are.

How did I become a transformational leader? It happened partly because I demonstrated transformational outcomes in my family, my education, my work, and my community involvement. But I also became a transformational leader because that was what I said I was. And I invited my friends and the public to hold me accountable as a transformational leader.

5. Take action toward your goals.

Transformation begins with action. Taking action toward your goals is essential for turning your aspirations into tangible outcomes. A good starting point is breaking down your goals into smaller, manageable tasks or action steps. Breaking them down makes them less overwhelming and allows you to focus on taking one step at a time.

Once you've broken these down, the next step is to set your priorities and determine which tasks or actions are the most important and will have the greatest impact on moving you closer to your goals. Develop a clear and detailed plan of action based on these identified priorities, and then stay organized and commit to taking regular and consistent action toward your goals. Even small steps taken consistently can lead to significant progress over time.

Make it a habit to work on your goals daily or weekly, depending on your timeframe and their urgency. Anticipate and prepare for potential obstacles or challenges that may come up, and identify strategies to help you overcome these obstacles. Adopt a resilient mindset and view challenges as opportunities for growth.

Don't be afraid to seek support from others along the way. Reach out to mentors, coaches, or friends who can provide guidance, accountability, or resources. Surround yourself with a supportive network that encourages and motivates you to stay on track, and make a habit of monitoring your progress toward your goals. Assess what is working well and what needs adjustment, and celebrate your milestones and accomplishments along the way, in order to maintain your motivation and momentum.

Conclusion: Accountable Leadership

An accountable leader must always be ready for their leadership to be assessed in terms of promised outcomes. Driven by integrity and purpose, accountable leaders share their mission and goals with the world. When leaders exhibit this behavior, they are powerful. Their impact can be immediate or can take generations, but through their intentions, they create the possibility for meaningful change. This change starts for all organizations with their leaders' own words, and when leaders can rely on each other, they can imagine and create their future.

PART II

Leading the Team

A team is any group of individuals who work together toward a common goal or objective. Team members typically have complementary skills and expertise that enable them to collaborate and achieve outcomes that would be difficult or impossible to achieve alone.

Effective teams are characterized by open communication, mutual respect, shared goals and values, and a willingness to work toward a common vision. They may be composed of individuals with different backgrounds, experiences, and perspectives, but they are united by a common purpose and a commitment to achieving a shared outcome.

Teams can be found in a variety of settings, such as in the workplace, in sports, in community organizations, and in educational institutions. They can be temporary or ongoing in nature and may be structured in different ways, depending on the nature of the tasks or projects at their center.

Contemporary team leadership is centered on effectively leading and managing teams in today's dynamic and complex work environments.

Except in cases of friendship, and within some volunteer and religious activities, teams typically exist within larger organizational contexts. These organizations have bigger goals to achieve and therefore create specialized teams to handle the different aspects of the whole. Such teams could include the customer service, sales, and technical support departments, as well as policy or program implementation teams.

In many organizations, teams are interdependent, meaning that they require input from other teams to effectively deliver on their objectives. Let's take the example of a medium-sized city bakery.

To start the day's work, the production team would require input from the sales team to know how many loaves of bread to bake in order to meet demand. The head of procurement in the same bakery would also need input from the sales and production teams to project demand for inputs over the month so ingredients could be sourced in bulk, to qualify for a discount from the suppliers. Likewise, the finance team would need input from the sales team to know which customers to invoice, and for how many loaves of bread. The procurement team would also need the finance team to pay for the supplies, without which there would be no flour and yeast to bake the loaves of bread, the orders brought in by the sales team notwithstanding.

From this example, we see that modern team leadership requires collaboration and effective communication among team members and with other parties both internal and external to the organization. If these collaborations are to be effective, team leaders need to empower their team members by delegating responsibilities, providing autonomy, and fostering a culture of trust. They need to encourage personal growth and professional development by offering opportunities for skill enhancement and continuous learning, so that the members can make consistent and correct decisions. The leaders also need to support their team members' aspirations and provide coaching and feedback to help them reach their full potential.

Transformational team leaders recognize the importance of emotional intelligence in building strong relationships and promoting a positive team culture. They are empathetic, understanding, and aware of their team members' emotions and needs. They create a psychologically safe environment where team members feel comfortable expressing themselves, taking risks, and contributing their unique perspectives. Having the opposite of this environment can be quite bad.

Once, as a teenager living in California, I worked at a car wash so that I could supplement my family's income. The small facility had been opened by a business owner from the new immigrant community who was chasing the American dream. The organization's culture demanded that everything had to be done per the supervisors' instructions. There was no room for other employees to think or innovate, and we remained silent even in moments when what we had to say might prevent future problems. None of us would dare to speak out and contradict an order that had been issued by the supervisors.

One day, a mechanic brought in a car he had just repaired to get an engine wash before delivering the vehicle to the owner. Unfortunately, one of the supervisors mistakenly exchanged the engine-wash ticket with a body-wash ticket that was meant for a different client's new BMW. Duncan, a fellow car-wash attendant, saw what had happened but kept quiet because he wasn't supposed to contradict the supervisor. The outcome? The BMW got a beautiful engine wash that resulted in a short circuit in some engine components that weren't supposed to have gotten wet. The car wash was subsequently slapped with an expensive repair bill, and that's how it came to be closed down. Everyone lost their jobs: Duncan and the supervisor in question included.

While instructions and procedures are important for successful operations, simple flexibility in work processes is necessary as well. For example, Duncan speaking out despite the fear of contradicting the supervisor, or the supervisor demonstrating tolerance from the rank-and-file staff despite existing rules and procedures, would have saved the car wash and earned everyone another day at work.

This experience hammered into my young head the importance of awareness in situations where quick decision-making is needed in order to save a situation, as well as the beauty of encouraging team leaders to be flexible and adaptable. After thinking about it over time, I have become convinced that to lead a team well, a leader needs to think about three things: the dignity (or psychological safety) of the team, empathy, and inclusion. These three categories form the rules that will be discussed in this section of the book.

Dignity

ENTERING KENYA THROUGH THE LIBOI BORDER

A ll through my life, I have had experiences that have caused me to reflect on the question of psychological safety. Of course, in most of those instances, I was not thinking about psychological safety in the same terms that I now use to define it. Today, I think about psychological safety as the shared belief held by team members that they are allowed to take risks, express their concerns and ideas, speak up if they have questions, and own up to their mistakes without fearing negative consequences. Earlier in life, I experienced a lack of psychological safety simply as a denial of dignity. This denial of dignity is essentially what a team that lacks psychological safety also experiences.

One personal example of this occurred when I was a boy, as my family and I were crossing the Liboi border into Kenya. At the time, there was no easy way out of Somalia. Escaping through the port city of Kismayo was out of the question, so we'd had to make the harrowing journey through the burning cities of Somalia and hope for the best. We traveled through Dhoobley, Qooqaani, and Afmadow, just to name a few.

Eventually, we reached Liboi. Crossing the border into Kenya felt like a big achievement. We had successfully navigated our way through Somalia's war zones. We had withstood hunger and thirst. We had overcome the many obstacles that stood between us and the land that was the object of our hope. At last, we felt free.

My sisters hugged each other and cried, unable to withstand the emotional strain any longer. I felt as if a large burden that I had been carrying for ages had been heaved off my shoulders. The mental anguish my family and I had suffered in the two months since the war had broken out had turned us into short-tempered people, the kind who viewed everything with skepticism and mistrust. But in this moment, I trusted that crossing over to Kenya would give us a second chance at life.

As we approached the Kenyan town of Dadaab, the sprawling refugee camp came into view. The vast expanse of white tents seemed to stretch on forever, the overwhelming sight filling me with both hope and apprehension. It was hard to fathom that this would be our new home, a place where we would seek solace and safety after the horrors we had endured. As our truck rumbled along the dusty roads leading to the camp, I couldn't help but notice the sheer number of people we passed, the countless faces etched with weariness and longing. The camp seemed like a city unto itself, teeming with life and yet marred by the hardships of displacement. It was a stark reminder that we were not alone in our struggle.

The Liboi border post was a small immigration facility set up in a remote and inhospitable area in what had previously been Kenya's North Frontier District (NFD). The compound consisted of three short trees and an old wooden office block. Behind the block were a few makeshift houses, made of iron sheets, that housed the security officers on duty at the post. At least, that was the part that was visible to me from the queue.

Around the camp were armed Administration Police (AP) and members of the Kenyan military. While some of them conducted searches of the refugees, to ensure none were armed or attempting to smuggle weapons into Kenya, others stood by on guard or leaned against the walls of the nearby structures, their guns strapped over their shoulders. The inspection for arms was necessary, one soldier explained to my dad, who, though complying, jokingly inquired about the exercise.

"You see, there are good Somalis and, as you have already seen by now, there are some who aren't nice at all," said one soldier. He ran his hands along Dad's flanks as if hoping to feel a gun tucked away there.

"I understand that," replied Dad. "But do you still expect the not-so-nice ones to cross the border through the legally designated routes?"

"Yes and no," replied the soldier, now moving on to search my brother Abdirizak. "You see, you can't get to the refugee camps without security clearance. There might be bad elements who intend to register as refugees and then use weapons to carry out criminal activities here. We have to prevent that. However, we aren't oblivious to the porous nature of our borders, which means criminals can cross into Kenya at any point along the several hundreds of miles of open fields that we call our borders." As the soldier explained all this, he moved on down the queue.

His words left me wondering what the purpose of the body search was, if anyone could cross over at any point. Was it intended to be just another small humiliation? Was it just a way for someone to chip away at our already nonexistent sense of safety? Were we not owed dignity?

About six hours after we'd reached Liboi, at a quarter to four in the afternoon, we were allowed into the presence of the officers from the United Nations High Commissioner for Refugees (UNHCR). We were then directed to a registration center, where we would be processed and assigned a tent in one of the designated areas.

Inside the center, the line snaked its way around the makeshift desks manned by aid workers who were diligently recording information and distributing identification cards. The atmosphere was a mixture of chaos and desperation, with people clamoring for attention and trying to assert their presence in a sea of anonymity.

Finally, it was our turn to be registered. A weary-looking aid worker greeted us, her eyes filled with a combination of fatigue and boredom. She asked for our names, ages, and places of origin, ticking off boxes on a form with practiced efficiency. I couldn't help but feel a pang of disappointment as we became just another set of data, our lives reduced to mere statistics.

The aid worker handed us the identification cards that would serve as our lifeline in this new environment: each one a flimsy piece of plastic that bore its bearer's photograph and a string of alphanumeric characters that would forever be associated with that person's identity as a refugee. It was a bitter reminder of how easily our individuality had been stripped away, replaced by a system that categorized us in terms of our displacement. If I lost the paper, I would be lost from the global radar, and so would my family members, if they lost theirs.

As we made our way toward our assigned tent, I couldn't help but reflect on the loss of dignity we had experienced. Our dreams, aspirations, and unique stories seemed inconsequential in this new reality. We were reduced to the collective, a mass of displaced individuals seeking refuge and survival. It was a painful realization that the world saw us as a burden, as a problem to be managed, rather than as individuals deserving of respect and compassion.

Inside the tent, the heat was stifling, and the air hung heavy with a sense of despair. We unpacked what little belongings we had managed to bring with us, creating makeshift beds and arranging our meager possessions. The tent became a symbol of our transient existence, a temporary sanctuary that offered little in terms of comfort or privacy.

Days turned into weeks, and weeks into months, as we settled into the rhythm of life in the camp. We lined up for food distributions, stood in long queues for water, and navigated the complexities of communal living. The days blurred together, a monotonous cycle of survival that tested our resilience and hope.

Yet, amid the challenges and indignities, there were moments of connection and resilience that reminded me of our shared humanity. In the evenings, many of us gathered around a small fire, sharing stories and songs, and finding solace in our common experiences. We formed bonds with fellow refugees, creating a sense of community that transcended the confines of our circumstances.

As I think of it today, I realize that while our dignity may have been denied in the eyes of the world, it was something we could never truly lose. It resided in the strength and resilience that carried us through each day, in our determination to rebuild our lives and reclaim our identities. Our worth could not be reduced to numbers on a piece of paper or the circumstances that forced us to seek refuge. Even so, I didn't know it then.

SAN DIEGO SOCIAL SERVICES: DENYING OUR FAMILY DIGNITY

My refugee number was not to be the only indignity I would experience in my life. Months later, after going through the processes that finally brought us to America—and after having stayed in Denver for several months with relatives—my family and I found ourselves in San Diego. We were trying to make our life there.

Unlike in Denver, where institutions functioned as they should and social support recipients were treated with much dignity, much of the public assistance we received at San Diego fell short of our expectations. This was perhaps on account of the huge immigrant population in San Diego. I still recall how humiliating it was for a family to be recipients of welfare assistance in San Diego, no matter how deserving. One day Mom almost broke down after arriving home from an unsuccessful attempt to get help. I loved my mom so much, and I didn't like the look of frustration that had developed on her face.

I joined my mother in the process of seeking assistance, a long-drawn-out effort that took over a month. The fact is that we needed assistance urgently because we were running out of essential supplies. We also needed medical insurance cards as soon as possible.

I remember how the whole effort began. My sister Fardowsa called the local Department of Health and Human Services, only to get hung up on even before anyone listened to her case. We couldn't believe it. Disgusting as their treatment of her was, we decided to treat the incident as a technical hitch and tried to think of some excuses for what had happened, if only to reassure ourselves of our human dignity.

After considering the situation, we resolved to visit the office in person the following day. Fardowsa, my brother Abdirizak, and I accompanied Mom to the offices in San Diego. After waiting in the queue for a couple of hours, we were served by a caseworker. The encounter lasted less than a minute. The caseworker gave us an appointment for two weeks down the line.

At no point was any sensitivity shown for our needs, especially the urgent need for medical cards to get health checkups, made even more urgent at a time when Mom was struggling with her high blood pressure. We returned home completely frustrated. Yes, this was America, but the treatment we had received on this day was the same as the indifference demonstrated at times by camp administrators at the Dadaab and Utange refugee camps back in Kenya, if not as severe.

Deep within, I swore that if God ever gave me a chance to work with the needy, or to serve any group of people, I would care enough to listen and not just apply the same template response to every case. I would serve them as dignified people. I wouldn't allow stereotypes and blanket generalizations to cloud my judgment of who people are, and I wouldn't ignore their pleas for help.

The two weeks that followed felt like a century of waiting. We spent the little cash we had on us. We returned to the Department of Health and Human Services for our scheduled meeting. The purpose of the meeting was to determine our eligibility to receive food stamps and medical and cash assistance. As we were not the only family being served, we sat in the waiting room for almost three and a half hours. We could not eat or drink at the offices, as bringing food and drinks to the premises was prohibited.

Finally, we got to meet with the same caseworker we had seen before, in her office. Once again, she looked quite businesslike with everything she did: no expression of humanity accompanying her delivery of service. Perhaps she had listened to cases far worse than ours, or maybe the sheer volume and routine nature of the work had eaten up her heart. She was just there, seemingly immune to the plight of all the people that she was employed to serve. Without much ado, the strenuous interview process began.

She took down our details once again as she had done the first time we met. It would have been easier for her to pull out the file from the shelf, and I wondered if standing up was perhaps too much work for her. We gave her every detail she needed, and she put the information down in a new file. She didn't look up all the while but kept mumbling the questions while looking down, for the most part, at the forms she was filling in.

One of the most humbling questions I recall Mom being asked was how much money she had in the house. She said she didn't have any—which was indeed true. We were thereafter certified eligible for public assistance. This was to be the beginning of a long process of submitting monthly reports on whether any material changes had taken place at home. Such changes included whether a new child had been born, anyone had died, we had received any cash, someone had started work, or anyone had left or started school, among other issues.

From my understanding, the purpose of any public assistance program should be to help people get back on their own feet. Its goal should be to provide short-term assistance in times of crisis, as opposed to perpetuating long-term dependence. During such times of need, families that depend on public assistance should be treated with the dignity that they deserve.

It is the poor service given to needy families—service without dignity—and the demeaning treatment my family received at the welfare offices in San Diego that I first thought of when I determined that I would do better. Decades after the experiences I have described here, when I became a public servant, I shared with others my family's experience with an insensitive government. I challenged my team to remember the dignity of the people we serve.

After the humiliating experience of looking for social service help, we in my family set out to do whatever we could to reclaim the family's dignity. We decided we would work at whatever job opportunity presented itself. As a way of reducing our reliance on social welfare, my brother Abdirizak and I found jobs as part-time guards with a private security firm. We took up the job and did it passionately, knowing that our lives depended on it.

Those immediate actions were important. But even more important were the lessons I carried into any community service work I did. I would like to think that every person I have had the pleasure of leading can attest to the fact that they have had the freedom to speak their minds. Their thoughts and feelings have been considered. They have been treated as people, not stereotypes. They have been allowed their human dignity.

LEAD IN DIGNITY

The story of my family's experience on the border of Somalia and Kenya reveals that refugees are in search of physical and psychological safety. Refugees flee conflicts where their lives are at risk, and they look for sanctuary. They want to be treated as human beings.

In February 2022, Russia invaded Ukraine. New to the Biden administration and recently arrived at the State Department in Washington, DC, I knew from experience that there would be refugees from the war. Women, children, the elderly, and the disabled would be among those who fled the violence for their physical safety.

A unique set of refugees in this crisis were global migrants who had moved to Ukraine for their education or employment. I was personally aware of educated refugees who had fled the war in Somalia and other African crises in search of peace and stability in Ukraine. When the war in Ukraine began, not all nations and international agencies viewed these people as legitimate refugees. Barriers were being put up that kept these immigrants from finding safety in neighboring countries.

In my first days at the State Department, I spoke up for the dignity of these refugees, and I was disheartened to find racist attitudes toward African refugees within the United States government. I persisted, advocating for the Biden-Harris administration to call publicly and forcefully for the equal treatment of all refugees.

On February 28, 2022, the U.S. State Department's Bureau of African Affairs issued a statement that said, "The United States is coordinating with UN agencies and other governments to ensure every individual, including African students, crossing from Ukraine to seek refuge is treated equally—regardless of race, religion, or nationality." One month later, President Joe Biden visited refugees from Ukraine who'd found safety in Poland. Reflecting on this meeting in a March 26, 2022, post published on his official Facebook account, he said, "You don't need to speak the same language to feel the roller-coaster of emotions in their eyes." Ensuring the basic human dignity of all is an intangible challenge, but implementing a policy to welcome all refugees equally is a tangible solution.

This story of Ukrainian refugees focused on physical safety, but as I mentioned earlier, you cannot address the question of dignity without talking about psychological safety. This concept was initially discovered by Professor Amy Edmondson during her PhD research and has gained significant recognition in recent years. It first emerged as an element vital to the understanding of the relationship between teamwork, error-making, and overall team performance.

As she noted, psychological safety is not merely an individual trait; rather, it is an emergent property of any group. It shapes the learning behavior of the team and subsequently influences team performance, which in turn affects organizational success. In fact, research has shown that team members who work closely together tend to exhibit similar levels of psychological safety, highlighting its collective nature.

Psychological safety within teams yields numerous benefits. Firstly, it enhances team members' engagement and motivation by creating an environment where their contributions are valued and where they feel comfortable speaking up without fear of reprisal. Secondly, it facilitates better decision-making processes, as individuals are more inclined to voice their opinions and concerns. This inclusivity results in a broader range of perspectives being considered, leading to improved outcomes. Thirdly, it fosters a culture of continuous learning and growth, as team members feel safe to share their mistakes and learn from them, creating a foundation for innovation and resilience.

Extensive research, including Edmondson's original work and Google's Project Aristotle (a study focused on identifying the elements that make up a successful team), has consistently demonstrated the substantial impact that psychological safety has on team performance, innovation, creativity, and learning. The latter project, employing sophisticated statistical models and extensive variables, concluded that team composition mattered less than the quality of teamwork, with psychological safety being the most influential factor. Conversely, the absence of psychological safety has been shown to have detrimental effects on employee well-being, leading to increased stress, burnout, job turnover, and reduced organizational performance.

Over the years, academics have identified important nuances in the concept of psychological safety. For one, its significance becomes more pronounced in work environments that demand discretionary decision-making, particularly in creative, novel, or highly collaborative tasks. Furthermore, given the rise of hybrid work arrangements, managers need to expand their understanding of psychological safety to accommodate the unique challenges and dynamics of remote collaboration. Additionally, researchers are exploring the interaction between psychological safety and diversity within teams, with initial evidence suggesting that high psychological safety can unlock the full potential of diverse expertise, positively impacting team performance.

No matter what discoveries the future holds, the recognition of psychological safety as a fundamental element in team dynamics has already transformed our understanding of effective teamwork. Its influence on engagement, decision-making, continuous learning, and overall organizational performance is well-documented. As organizations strive for success, cultivating psychological safety within teams should be a priority, as it leads to a culture that nurtures individual well-being, harnesses the power of diverse perspectives, and promotes innovation and growth.

PRIORITIZE THE SAFETY OF THE TEAM

Dignity is the first step in connecting with people. This is true at a personal level but also true for organizational leaders. The stories I've shared from my life demonstrate the challenges inherent in leading with dignity. What alternate treatment by others might have afforded my father dignity at the Liboi border crossing? What could the social services worker in San Diego have done differently to see the dignity of my mother? Or viewed another way: How can a leader of a nation make sure that refugees feel physically and psychologically safe? Dignity is not a one-time experience but an ongoing approach to people.

Research conducted by Donna Hicks, an associate professor at Harvard University's Weatherhead Center for International Affairs and the author of *Leading with Dignity*, has deeply impacted my understanding of this topic. Like me, Hicks got her professional start as a peacebuilder, leading dialogues focused on resolving international conflicts. She saw that deep conflicts between people could not be resolved with new ideas or clever solutions. Conflict resolution required addressing the emotional hurt that parties carried within them. People remember times when they are treated unequally and when their inherent worth is not valued. Families often pass this hurt down, generation to generation. Leaders need to heal this pain, to help people reclaim their dignity, so that they can then make peace.

Hicks offers the following approach to leading with dignity. Her wisdom can be helpful to you whether you need healing yourself or are helping to bring peace to someone else. First, a person's identity needs to be accepted, no matter who they are. People need to be recognized for what they uniquely offer, and they need to be acknowledged: that is, heard and seen. People who are led with dignity are given both a sense of belonging and the freedom to live their lives in hope and possibility. Hicks understands the necessity of feeling safe and being treated fairly. Individuals need the time and space to be understood. Finally, incorporating accountability into leadership allows leaders to apologize and to forgive when mistakes are made.

In addition to Hicks's suggestions, I offer the following guidelines to help you respect the dignity of people you lead:

1. **Make it clear that what team members have to say matters.**

In many teams, there is a prevailing inclination for people to hold back their ideas and opinions, choosing silence over speaking up. It is crucial for leaders who want to counteract this instinct to create an environment that encourages and values individual voices. By doing so, you can unlock the untapped potential and unique perspectives that each individual brings to the table.

Find ways to explicitly and compellingly convey to employees that their viewpoints and input truly matter. By articulating the importance of their team members' contributions, leaders can demonstrate how their voices directly influence the outcomes of the work. Whether through innovative ideas, diverse perspectives, or critical feedback, each employee has a valuable role to play in driving the success of the team and the organization as a whole. By fostering an environment where everyone's voice is heard and valued, organizations can tap into a wealth of untapped potential and foster a sense of ownership and engagement among employees.

2. **Admit that you are not perfect.**

One effective way for leaders to promote a culture of contribution is by acknowledging their own fallibility. When leaders openly acknowledge their mistakes and share how they have learned from them, it sets a powerful example for others to do the same. By modeling the behavior they want to see in their team, leaders create a space in which it's safe to be vulnerable, where employees feel comfortable sharing their thoughts, ideas, and concerns. This requires leaders to exhibit respect for all team members, to be open to feedback, and to be willing to take calculated risks. By normalizing vulnerability, leaders create an environment where growth, innovation, and continuous improvement flourish.

3. Resolve conflicts in constructive ways.

Conflicts are a natural part of working in teams, and resolving them constructively can lead to stronger relationships and improved collaboration. By addressing conflicts promptly, encouraging open communication, and seeking mutually beneficial solutions, you can foster a positive team dynamic and create an environment where conflicts are seen as opportunities for growth and learning. When conflicts arise, take the time to understand the perspective of every individual involved in the conflict. Listen actively and empathetically to each person's point of view without judgment, and ensure that all of the involved parties get a fair opportunity to express themselves fully.

Identify areas of agreement or shared goals among the conflicting parties, and emphasize these commonalities, to foster a sense of unity and collaboration. Finding common ground can serve as a starting point for resolving the conflict and for finding a solution that meets the needs of all involved. In more complex or escalated conflicts, consider involving a neutral third party to facilitate the resolution process. This could be a team leader, a representative from the Human Resources department, or an external mediator. The mediator can help guide the discussion, ensure fair participation, and assist the team members in exploring potential solutions.

Have the conflicting parties brainstorm and generate multiple potential solutions to the conflict. Encourage creativity and open-mindedness during this process. Consider the pros and cons of each solution, and evaluate them based on their feasibility and their potential to address the underlying issues. Ask the conflicting parties to articulate their underlying interests rather than focusing solely on their stated positions. Understanding the motivations and needs behind each person's stance makes it easier to find creative solutions that address those interests.

From there, facilitate a discussion and negotiation process designed to reach a solution that all parties can agree on. Encourage compromise and emphasize the importance of finding a resolution that benefits the team as a whole. Document the agreed-upon solution to ensure clarity and accountability.

Once a resolution has been reached, follow up with the team members involved to ensure that the agreed-upon solution is implemented effectively. Monitor the progress and provide support as needed. Regularly check in with the team to ensure that the conflict has been fully resolved and to address any lingering issues or concerns.

Conclusion: Leadership with Dignity

The most fundamental practice that teams need to succeed is the practice of leadership with dignity: that is, being led by a leader who respects each individual. Leaders succeed when they value what makes each person unique, and leaders fail when they dehumanize people, reduce them to a collective, or demean them by viewing them as a problem to be solved or by ignoring them. When leaders treat people as humans, everyone does better. Good leaders meet individuals as equals and create safety for all. This is an outcome that helps organizations and leaders to operate beyond the limits of their experiences and biases.

Empathy

EXPERIENCING EXTRAORDINARY
KINDNESS IN DENVER

It was a chilly winter day on January 26, 1994, when my family and I landed in Denver, Colorado. Snow covered the ground, and as we disembarked from the plane, I glanced at my sister Kowsar and my mom. They were equally bewildered by the sight. Kowsar, in her innocence, insisted that the white substance was nothing more than salt. Little did we know, this day would mark the beginning of a life-changing chapter for us: one filled with acts of compassion performed by a few remarkable individuals.

Awaiting our arrival at the Denver airport were our relatives Yusuf, his wife, Anab, and two extraordinary souls named James and Dorothy, from the Church World Service: a faith-based organization that sponsors refugees and whose work includes providing assistance to refugees. As we approached them, I was overwhelmed with emotion; I could feel the weight of uncertainty lifting from our shoulders. Our temporary shelter was to be Yusuf and Anab's home, where we would reside while the Church World Service tirelessly searched for a suitable place to accommodate our family of fourteen.

Life at Yusuf and Anab's house felt like a dream. I couldn't help but marvel at the luxurious lifestyle they enjoyed. We'd come from a place where hot water for bathing was a luxury and fetching drinking water was a daily chore, and the abundance of clean, safe water flowing from the taps was a revelation. Microwaves warmed our food, and an enormous refrigerator kept our food fresh. This was the America I had only heard about before, and now I was experiencing it firsthand.

Dorothy and James also played pivotal roles in helping us settle into our new home and creating a sense of comfort. Dorothy, almost like a guardian angel, visited us weekly, taking us on outings to Denver's shopping malls. Each time, we returned home with presents that warmed our hearts, including enough fresh fruit to feed our entire family.

I often wondered if Dorothy was an employee or a volunteer of the Church World Service. Regardless, her kindness knew no bounds. It was through Dorothy's efforts that we became connected with an English as a Second Language (ESL) teacher who came to our home after school to teach us English. I vividly remember this teacher, Valarie, urging me to learn several new words each day. Armed with my newfound vocabulary, I soon walked into school feeling like a genius.

For his part, James took a keen interest in helping my family and me integrate into Denver. Not only did he purchase my first pair of everyday sneakers, he also brought me multiple pairs of sports shoes, basketball jerseys, and even a basketball. What struck me most about James was his willingness to drop everything and play basketball with us. Unlike many busy American adults, James made time for sports. It was during one of these games that he introduced me to my first Gatorade, a drink that tasted to me like pure joy.

One of our most significant milestones was purchasing a used Toyota Camry, using money contributed by each family member. In this way, we were finally able to relieve Dorothy of her weekly trips to the grocery store to bring us fruit. Walking to the bus stop and relying on public transportation had become tiresome, and we'd longed for the freedom to explore our new surroundings. After almost a year in the U.S., my brother Abdirizak had obtained his driver's license, and he became our designated driver.

My brother Wali, having driven for more than two decades in Africa, had soon realized that driving in the U.S. was an entirely different experience. Traffic rules, weather conditions, and even the direction of traffic were new challenges to overcome. In Kenya and Somalia, for example, he had driven right-hand vehicles, keeping to the left on the road; here, driving meant operating a left-hand vehicle and keeping to the right.

Dorothy and James helped us to get used to these changes. All through the process, Dorothy never complained about driving us around. James never tired of giving us his time.

Even today, I think about the acts of compassion that Yusuf, Anab, Dorothy, and James demonstrated. As we faced adversity, their unwavering support and genuine kindness provided us with the strength to persevere. They taught us the importance of extending a helping hand to those in need, regardless of background or circumstances. These people who showed us compassion forever touched our hearts, instilling within us the belief that even in the toughest of times, there are angels among us who are ready to offer a guiding hand.

A JOURNEY OF SELF-DISCOVERY, THROUGH A MOTHER'S COMPASSION

My family arrived in Denver to a warm welcome, but relationships with our neighbors made it difficult to stay there (something I will talk about more in the first section of Part IV: Leading the Community). So, after a year, our mother moved our family to San Diego. The vibrant Somali community in our new neighborhood of City Heights made us feel like we belonged. Determined to pursue my thirst for knowledge, I looked forward to enrolling at Crawford High School. However, I knew that before diving into other academic pursuits, I would have to take English classes there, to enhance my language skills. English was not only the language of instruction but also the key to integration and success in American life.

My memories of life at Crawford High School are vivid, and I recall the challenges of trying to integrate with other communities. There were moments when students from other backgrounds would face criticism for considering friendship with Somali students. Despite our efforts to remain composed in the face of misconceptions about our way of life, street fights with Hispanic and African American gang members occasionally occurred, reinforcing negative stereotypes about the Somali community.

During my time in Denver, I had picked up some English words, mostly through playing basketball. Like any group of peers, we created our own language and gestures, using common English words in unique ways that only we understood. Unfortunately, this included the use of inappropriate language and expressions that disguised themselves as ordinary communication.

As someone learning English as a second language, I unintentionally brought these obscenities from the basketball court into the classroom, much to the disappointment of my teachers and fellow students. Consequently, I faced reprimands from teachers, and my female classmates hesitated to interact with me, fearing I might use scandalous words. I grew dejected and withdrew from participating in class discussions and conversations outside the classroom, unsure of the meaning of the words that would escape my lips.

Being surrounded by a large Somali population in San Diego didn't help the situation. Despite our teachers' best efforts to help us learn English, we Somali students often found ourselves conversing in our native language as soon as the teacher left the room. We would rush out of our classrooms during breaks, shouting in Somali, Somalia's national language. It was partly an act of teenage rebellion, a resistance to the very courses that were designed to help us. We didn't realize that we were hindering our progress in mastering the language that was vital for our survival, integration, and growth in America.

Like many of my Somali friends, I struggled academically. This resulted in poor grades and a shattered spirit. I soon realized that, although I was an avid reader and understood the concepts taught in class, my poor language skills prevented me from expressing myself effectively and demonstrating my understanding. I doubted that I could pass exams even if they were administered orally.

I began to regret not taking advantage of the free English language classes that had been offered at the refugee camps in Kenya. Though those classes were not professionally graded, they'd provided valuable advance help for coping with academic work and social life in America. I felt as though I had missed a crucial part of camp experience by prioritizing soccer over education when I was there. It was a case of poor decision-making: my actions had been driven by passion rather than purpose. Living as a refugee had been the lowest point in my life, and hope seemed like an elusive dream. This way of thinking had prevented me from making a choice that would have benefited my future.

Thankfully, amid my struggles with learning English in San Diego, I found solace and acceptance on the basketball court. My contributions to the game, made possible by my height advantage, gained recognition from my peers. Everyone wanted me on their team, and this gave me a sense of purpose. Escaping to the court became a way to cope with my feelings of inadequacy in the classroom. Whenever I received poor grades, I longed for a break and a chance to reassure myself that I still had value somewhere: in the game.

This quest for meaning unfortunately led me down a path of regrettable decisions. I prioritized sports over academic work and ended up severely dislocating an ankle during a basketball game. The injury forced me to stay away from the court for a time, but my obsession with playing pushed me to return before my ankle had fully healed.

The consequences were devastating, and it took nearly a year for me to recover from my injury. Being away from basketball stirred up even more questions about who I was and the circumstances in which I found myself. What did I truly want to do and achieve? I was growing tired of playing catch-up in every aspect of my life.

My mother and elder siblings noticed the changes in me and encouraged me to move away from sports and distractions, and to focus on my education. Mom became more attentive to my feelings, asking about my school experiences: what I had learned and whether I needed any special assistance. We started speaking English in most of our conversations at home, creating a safe environment for my sisters and me to practice the language without fear of criticism. My brother Wali even offered to hire a tutor, although it never came to that because by that time, I was already showing significant improvement in my academic performance. I realized I was finally on the right track to academic success. This was partially thanks to my injured ankle, but mostly, thanks to the compassion I was shown by my mother and my family members.

To further enhance my English skills, I enrolled in an after-school ESL program run by the International Rescue Committee, an organization whose humanitarian work includes providing support to refugees. This program played a vital role in helping me develop my language competence. Through my mother's compassion and the support of my family, I began to redefine myself. I realized the importance of education and the role it played in shaping my future. Along this journey, I also learned the significance of compassion itself. It was through my mother's understanding and encouragement that I found the strength to overcome obstacles and strive for academic success.

Today, I know for a fact that compassion is a universal language that transcends cultural and linguistic barriers. I witnessed firsthand how compassion could transform lives and bridge gaps between communities. The kindness and understanding I received from my family and friends helped me understand the value of extending compassion to others, no matter what their background or circumstances.

LEAD WITH EMPATHY

In the many jobs I have taken, from my first role at McDonald's to my current position in President Biden's administration, I have seen that people love empathetic leaders. Many managers love the idea of leading in this way. However, very few people can define what it looks like to lead with empathy.

The definition of empathy is to understand, to be sensitive to, or to be aware of the feelings, thoughts, and experiences of others. According to a report published in 2022 by Development Dimensions International, a global leadership development and human resources consulting firm, empathy is the most important of all leadership skills. However, only 40 percent of people say that their team leaders are empathetic. That statistic shows that there is a huge gap between what people are looking for and what leaders are offering.

It also points to the fact that it is not an easy thing to lead with empathy. After all, it is not as if empathetic leadership is part of a college curriculum. The majority of the time, leaders get promoted to leadership roles based on how successful they are as individual contributors. That means they come into the office needing to learn a whole new set of skills. I know that because I have been there. I, too, had to learn emotional intelligence to complement my technical expertise.

Utilizing my emotional intelligence was a key factor in my success as deputy commissioner of the Minnesota DEED. In 2021, I helped craft and pass the state's largest bipartisan jobs bill. This groundbreaking legislation passed in the middle of the COVID-19 pandemic, at a time when the workforce was in upheaval. People were reaching out in desperation to the government for economic assistance to meet their basic needs. As a point of reference, in 2019, my state agency processed 150,000 applications for unemployment benefits. Through the pandemic, that number grew to over 1.3 million. To better listen to the needs of individuals, my colleagues and I organized weekly online meetings with community organizations and business leaders. In these meetings, I heard from the local level what impact the pandemic was having on individuals, and this helped me determine how my team should respond to these urgent needs.

In the spring of 2021, my empathic leadership skills were tested by partisan politics. At that time, I was working closely with legislative committees on jobs and economic development. The committee in the state House was chaired by a fellow Somali refugee and old friend, Representative Mohamud Noor: a member of the Democratic Party from Minneapolis. In the state Senate, the Republicans were in charge, and Senator Eric Pratt, a banker from the town next to my home city, chaired the committee. I respected both Representative Noor and Senator Pratt, but they had very different political philosophies. I studied their personalities, learned their leadership styles, and listened to their unique visions for the future.

Conflict can be frustrating, but is also an invitation to better understand the motivations of each individual. For example, one of these two legislators focused more on low-income workers and the biggest cities. The other focused more on businesses and suburbs and small towns. Paying attention to both sets of priorities led us to fund the Main Street

Economic Revitalization Program, which invests in the business districts of both big cities and small towns. The bill included loan programs for small businesses and free training opportunities for workers, including a Coursera educational partnership and a youth tech-jobs program. From this experience, I came to understand the need to appeal to the empathy in all leaders. Delays in passing legislation would have hurt both the low-income workers and the small business owners these leaders care about. Working together, we passed a nearly $500 million jobs bill with the support of both political parties.

Empathy has always been recognized as a valuable skill for leaders, but its significance has reached new heights in today's dynamic and challenging business landscape. Contrary to misconceptions, empathy is not a soft approach; it is a powerful tool that can drive significant business results. Recent research has shed light on the importance of empathy to various aspects of leadership, including innovation, retention, and overall team performance. Great leaders understand that empathy is a vital element in creating the conditions for engagement, satisfaction, and high performance.

Empathetic leaders genuinely care about their team members' well-being, including their emotional health, personal challenges, and lives outside of work. By employing empathy, leaders can establish meaningful connections with their team, offer support, understand their needs, build trust, and cultivate strong relationships. Leaders who lead with empathy, instead of focusing solely on business outcomes, connect with their team members on a deeper level and effectively respond to their needs, providing motivation, support, and comfort in times of distress.

Empathetic leaders foster a sense of purpose, community, and belonging within the team. They are able to create an environment where team members feel a sense of purpose and connection to a larger mission. They foster a sense of community, encouraging collaboration and teamwork. Empathetic leaders are perceptive and attentive, recognizing when their team members may need additional assistance or support. They proactively offer help and create an environment where individuals feel comfortable seeking guidance.

Empathy also makes a number of demands. It requires that you actively listen and be fully present. It requires that you truly hear your team members, making a conscious effort to be fully present and engaged when others are speaking. Empathy demands that you demonstrate genuine interest in understanding different perspectives and ideas.

In today's world, people are experiencing various forms of stress. Research indicates that mental health issues have escalated, leading to increased stress, anxiety, emotional exhaustion, and other challenges among employees. Moreover, personal lives are impacted by workplace stress, which affects relationships, sleep quality, and overall well-being. Employee performance and turnover rates, and customer experiences, also suffer as a result of workplace stress.

Empathetic leadership plays a vital role in addressing these challenges. It creates a safe space for employees to share their struggles, and it promotes mental well-being in the workplace. Studies have shown that the positive effects of empathetic leadership include increased innovation, higher employee engagement, improved work-life balance, and a more inclusive work environment. Empathetic leaders understand and relate to their team members' needs, concerns, and emotions. This understanding paves the way for a supportive and motivational work environment, contributing to improved employee engagement and productivity. Additionally, empathetic leadership encourages diverse viewpoints, fostering a culture of innovation and creativity. Effective communication, trust, and collaboration are nurtured, leading to improved conflict resolution and better decision-making.

Ultimately, empathetic leadership is not just about understanding others; it also drives organizational success by prioritizing the human aspect of leadership and by building meaningful connections. How, then, do you lead with empathy?

HUMANIZE TEAMS THROUGH LISTENING AND COMPASSION

Empathy is the act of practicing dignity in action with others. While dignity can be respected as a concept, empathy requires a real connection between people. Empathy requires thinking about, listening to, and feeling with another. Dorothy and James from Church World Service welcomed my family as strangers to their community, and they listened with empathy to our individual needs and responded by giving gifts and spending time with us. When I was struggling in school, my mother took the time to listen to my struggles and to help me take positive steps toward my self-improvement. Empathy exists between people.

If you want to build effective relationships, you need empathy. Your listening skills affect your team's performance. When a leader doesn't engage their team, problems go undiagnosed and potential solutions remain unspoken. Be courageous in your conversations; you can bring out the best traits in yourself and others. Share your purpose and your passion for the success of your team. Through empathic conversations, you can uncover what motivates your team members, provide them permission to lead, and celebrate their achievements.

Here are some steps you can take to become a more empathetic leader:

1. Know yourself.

Becoming an empathetic leader is a transformative journey that begins with developing strong self-awareness. It entails delving into your inner self and gaining a deep understanding of the factors that motivate you, as well as your temperament and personality style. It also involves recognizing your communication style, how you react to feedback, and how your values shape your behavior as a leader. The first step on this journey is to invest in your own personal and professional development. By dedicating time and effort to self-reflection and introspection, you can uncover your strengths, weaknesses, and areas for growth. This self-awareness serves as a foundation for adjusting your leadership style to meet the unique needs of your team members.

Bear in mind that while individual leaders are responsible for their own development, senior executives also have a critical role to play in cultivating empathetic leaders throughout the organization. These executives must allocate organizational resources to support initiatives focused on the development of self-awareness and empathy. This investment can take the form of training programs, coaching sessions, or workshops designed to enhance leadership skills and foster empathy.

Furthermore, senior executives must lead by example and model the behaviors they expect from other leaders. By demonstrating empathy in their interactions and decision-making, they set the tone for others to follow. It is not enough to simply talk about the importance of empathy; leaders must embody it in their everyday actions. They have to engage in caring conversations with managers who may be struggling to develop into empathetic leaders. These discussions provide executives an opportunity to understand any challenges or barriers their managers may be facing and to offer guidance and support to help them grow.

2. Seek to understand other people.

The second crucial aspect of empathetic leadership is developing a deep understanding of your team members. This involves honing your communication skills, adopting a curious mindset in conversations, and eschewing defensiveness or aggression. It also entails creating a safe environment, as within relationships, trust cannot thrive in the presence of fear. If you want to be an empathetic leader, it is paramount to build trust with your team members. They need to perceive you as being genuinely on their side and invested in their success. Demonstrating this commitment helps them feel safe and secure in their environment. It is vital that, as their leader, you convey that your role is not to harm or undermine them, but rather to support and empower them.

A good place to begin is by learning your team members' individual strengths, weaknesses, aspirations, and challenges. Take the time to come to know their unique perspectives, needs, and goals, so that you can tailor your leadership approach to better serve them. This understanding enables you to provide meaningful support, guidance, and opportunities for growth that align with their specific requirements.

Notably, effective communication plays a critical role in understanding your team members. By actively listening, asking thoughtful questions, and demonstrating genuine curiosity, you create a space for open dialogue and connection. When two people come together with empathy, something truly remarkable happens. It's no longer just a one-way street of understanding, but a reciprocal exchange where both parties understand each other. In such a relationship, people create a deep connection, one that fosters trust, respect, and an environment where individuals feel genuinely heard and valued. This dynamic isn't limited to just the leader's role; it extends to the entire team, where thoughtful exchanges become the cornerstone of an empathetic culture. In this space, with empathy flowing in all directions, relationships flourish and the collective strength of the team grows, paving the way for collaboration, innovation, and collective success.

3. Build a team through understanding.

Team composition plays a crucial role in ensuring the productivity of the team in question and the organization as a whole. This makes the team's composition an important determinant of success for any leader. When assembling a team, important considerations include first identifying the team's deliverables and then identifying the right set of skills and expertise to bring into the team. Each team member should bring a unique set of abilities and knowledge that complements those of other team members and contributes to the overall capabilities of the team.

To guarantee the success of your project, look for individuals who are enthusiastic about the initiative, willing to invest the necessary time and effort, and dedicated to achieving success. Let these things be underpinned by a commitment to include everyone who qualifies. As for the number of team members, consider that too small a team may lack diverse perspectives and expertise, while too large a team can lead to coordination challenges and decreased productivity. Find a balance that allows for effective collaboration and efficient decision-making.

Empathy is a powerful tool for building a team. You, as the team leader, hold the key to fostering an environment where each member feels valued and appreciated. Start by taking the time to truly understand each team member's strengths, weaknesses, and unique perspectives. Listen actively when they share their ideas, concerns, or aspirations. Empathize with their challenges and celebrate their successes. By doing so, you create a sense of belonging and trust within the team.

Encourage open and honest communication, making it clear that you are there to support and guide them. Show empathy when team members face personal or professional difficulties, and offer your assistance when needed. Building a team through understanding means recognizing that each individual brings something valuable to the table and each person's well-being matters.

Furthermore, create opportunities for team members to understand each other better. Foster a culture of collaboration, where they can learn from one another's experiences and expertise. Encourage activities that bond your team members and allow individuals to connect on a personal level; this will strengthen their relationships and increase their ability to work cohesively toward common goals.

4. Show compassion, and allow your team members to learn from their mistakes.

Empathetic leaders embody compassion and extend grace to others. They possess the ability to empathize and understand the perspectives of those they lead. Of course, it's also important to recognize that organizations have goals that need to be accomplished. Therefore, leaders must strike a balance between being compassionate and setting clear expectations that are communicated and understood by every team member. Many leaders tend to adopt an either/or mindset when it comes to leadership, focusing solely on *either* achieving outcomes *or* fostering relationships. However, I have found that it is possible to achieve both objectives by establishing a clear vision and direction for your team while working alongside them in a supportive and service-oriented manner, assisting them in accomplishing their goals.

I have noticed that in many organizations, it is the people who made mistakes and learned their lessons the hard way who get discharged from duty, leaving behind those who have never learned hard lessons. Take the example of Jeremy, a fresh graduate of journalism school whom I met in Washington, DC. He had just joined the media team as a cameraman in one of the country's leading media houses when he was placed on the schedule to work a press conference at the White House. He packed his camera in a hurry, swung his media accreditation badge around his neck, and hopped into the media van headed to the White House. When he finally unpacked the bag, he realized that he had left his two camera battery packs at his media desk at the TV station. He panicked inside but didn't hint to his reporter that anything was wrong, for fear of repercussions.

Quick thinking . . . and *bang!* A solution came to his mind. He could borrow a battery pack from another cameraperson at the event with the same camera make and model. This plan worked, and he quickly pushed the battery into his camera's socket and pushed the On button. The camera worked. What a relief! When President Biden got to the podium, Jeremy took another glance at his camera. The power was still on. After that, he followed the entire event from the camera's side screen, occasionally pausing to adjust the focus as circumstances necessitated.

It was only after the event that he realized that although he had turned on the camera, he never pressed Record, and so the entire event had gone unrecorded. Back at the station, he was sent home for professional negligence. Next, he lost his job. This hurt him, especially the thought that he'd lost both the job opportunity and the chance to include a leading media brand as an employer on his CV.

But to this day, Jeremy is the best cameraman that I know. I am certain that there are some mistakes that he will never repeat, including this one. He learned from his mistakes, and this made him a better person than he was before the White House press assignment. While empathetic leadership isn't about condoning negligence and costly mistakes, it does recognize the fact that people often learn from their mistakes and become invaluable assets to the teams they work in and to the larger organization.

5. Set boundaries.

Empathetic leaders possess the skill of establishing clear boundaries that benefit everyone involved. They understand the importance of communicating expectations, such as the number of hours that will be worked in a day or the inappropriateness of sending late-night emails to colleagues. When all team members have a clear understanding of work boundaries, including the rules and expectations that are in place, a sense of safety and freedom are created within the work environment. Boundaries serve as guardrails, preventing individuals from excessively sacrificing themselves to achieve a goal. Moreover, boundaries promote autonomy by clearly outlining what is permissible and what is not.

By setting clear boundaries, empathetic leaders enable individuals to have a better work-life balance, avoid burnout, and maintain their overall well-being. Empathetic leaders establish guidelines that foster a healthy and productive work environment, where individuals feel respected, supported, and empowered to perform at their best. In essence, empathetic leaders recognize that clear boundaries not only protect individuals from undue strain but also promote a sense of autonomy and enable them to understand what is expected of them. By establishing these boundaries, leaders contribute to a healthier and more productive work environment for all team members.

Conclusion: Empathetic Leadership

At its core, empathetic leadership revolves around being a leader who prioritizes the needs of others. It entails leaders being deeply attuned to the concerns and critical needs of their people and taking tangible actions that showcase their own genuine care and consideration for others. When leaders exhibit such behavior, the response from their team members is remarkable. They reciprocate with unwavering loyalty, trust, and commitment, which leads to enhanced productivity, innovation, and creativity. This is an outcome that any organization or leader would undoubtedly aspire to achieve.

PRACTICE 6

Inclusion

PRESIDENTIAL INITIATIVE FOR DEMOCRATIC RENEWAL

As a preteen, I wanted to stop the civil war that was emerging in my country, threatening to disrupt my life, which revolved around family, school, and soccer. It was during this tumultuous time of the war in Somalia that I first discovered my passion for peace activism. Despite my young age, I felt compelled to speak out against the violence invading my city. I joined a protest and marched with other young people to the city center to demand peace. As young people, we wanted our voices to be heard. But we were met by bullets flying toward us, and I fled, to protect the safety of my family.

Years later, as an adult, I found myself in a position where I could make a tangible impact on the world around me. This time around, my efforts could yield fruit. President Biden's Presidential Initiative for Democratic Renewal, launched in December 2021 at the first Summit for

Democracy, and the accompanying Year of Action (which I discussed in Practice 1: Integrity) presented an incredible opportunity to bring about change on a larger scale. I knew that this was a chance to prioritize the inclusion of young people in the work of shaping our society's future.

Under the auspices of the Presidential Initiative for Democratic Renewal, I worked alongside my colleagues across the federal government, including my friend Scott Warren of the United States Agency for International Development (USAID), who is also the author of *Generation Citizen: The Power of Youth in Our Politics*. Along with other passionate individuals, Scott and I, and our other colleagues, set out to launch the youth cohort as part of the summit, to serve as a prime example of inclusion. We recognized that the voices and perspectives of young people are vital to driving meaningful and sustainable change. We wanted to ensure that their voices were not only heard but also valued and integrated into the decision-making processes of the summit.

The journey was not without its challenges. We faced skeptics who questioned whether young people had the ability to contribute meaningfully to such important discussions. However, we remained steadfast in our belief that age should not be a barrier to participation and our conviction that the passion and fresh perspectives of young minds could lead to innovative solutions.

Through teamwork, dedication, and a shared vision, we were able to create a platform that empowered young people to be active agents of change. The summit helped organize a global movement in which government leaders, private-sector leaders, and civil-society leaders all participated, providing a space for young voices to be heard, ideas to be shared, and relationships to be forged. We fostered an environment that encouraged collaboration, diversity, and open dialogue.

The Summit for Democracy's youth cohort was hosted by the European Commission, the European Partnership for Democracy, the European Democracy Youth Network, AfricTivistes, and the governments of Ghana and Nepal. The cohort was inspiring. Young people from diverse backgrounds came together, shared their experiences, and offered unique insights into the pressing issues of our time. Their perspectives challenged traditional narratives and brought fresh ideas to the table. It was evident that their involvement added depth and richness to the conversations, leaving a lasting impact on the decisions made during the Summit for Democracy's Year of Action.

The inclusion of young people not only enriched the process but also created a sense of ownership and empowerment among the participants. They felt valued and respected, knowing that their voices carried weight in the shaping of the future. This sense of ownership translated into a newfound commitment to civic engagement and activism, inspiring many members to continue their work long after the work of the cohort concluded.

I am immensely proud of the journey we embarked on and the impact we were able to make. The launch of the youth cohort was a testament to the power of inclusion, demonstrating that when leaders create spaces for diverse voices to be heard, we unlock the potential for transformative change. This experience reaffirmed my belief in the importance of amplifying marginalized voices and ensuring that every individual—regardless of age, race, or background—has a seat at the table. If we dare to be bold as team leaders, the choices we make can serve as significant steps to building a more inclusive and equitable society. I remain committed to continuing this fight for inclusion, and to striving to create spaces where all voices are valued and every individual has the opportunity to contribute to a better world.

THE MURDER OF GEORGE FLOYD AND WHAT FOLLOWED

As a senior leader in Minnesota's response to the twin pandemics of COVID-19 and racial injustice, I was part of a leadership team at DEED that faced unprecedented challenges. My colleagues and I were tasked with a seemingly impossible mission: processing unemployment insurance claims during a time of immense uncertainty and distress. Little did we know that our work would soon intersect with the tragic murder of George Floyd, amplifying the urgency and importance of our efforts.

The pandemic had already plunged our state into a once-in-a-century crisis, with people dying of COVID-19, businesses shutting down, workers losing their jobs, and the economy spiraling downward. As countless individuals sought support and stability amid the chaos, my days were consumed by the overwhelming influx of unemployment claims, the urgent needs of businesses at risk of closing, and displaced workers urgently seeking new jobs and new skills. Our work was a constant battle against time as we labored to process claims efficiently, to ensure that those in need received their benefits on time.

Against this background, something else happened in Minnesota that had a major impact on my work. The crisis began on May 25, 2020, in Minneapolis, when George Floyd, a Black man, was arrested and then murdered by four police officers, including Derek Chauvin. George was forty-six, just a few years older than me. He'd come to Minnesota from Texas in 2014, just two years after I arrived. If George had been white, he would be alive today.

A video capturing the incident went viral, showing Chauvin kneeling on Floyd's neck for over nine minutes, despite Floyd's pleas that he couldn't breathe. The footage sent shockwaves across the world, exposing the systemic racism and police brutality that disproportionately affects Black communities.

The video sparked immediate outrage and ignited protests in Minneapolis, with protesters demanding justice for George Floyd and an end to police violence. As the news spread, demonstrations spread to cities across the United States and eventually around the globe. The moment became a rallying cry for the Black Lives Matter movement and a call to address the deep-rooted racism and systemic injustices that permeate society.

Protests erupted in cities large and small, with people from diverse backgrounds taking to the streets to express their anger and frustration. The demonstrations were predominantly peaceful, but instances of violence and looting also occurred, often carried out by a small minority of individuals who were taking advantage of the chaos. The demand for justice gained momentum, and all four officers involved in Floyd's arrest were eventually arrested and charged. Derek Chauvin faced charges of unintentional second-degree murder, third-degree murder, and second-degree manslaughter. The trials and legal proceedings that followed would become pivotal moments in the fight for justice.

As the protests continued, calls for police reform and for an end to racial profiling grew louder. Communities and activists demanded a reevaluation of policing practices, advocating for alternatives to armed law enforcement and urging greater accountability for officers who abuse their power. The movement extended beyond the streets, reaching into various sectors of society. Corporations, institutions, and individuals began to engage in introspection, questioning their own biases and privilege, and committing to anti-racist actions. The conversation around systemic racism became more prominent, leading to discussions about education, healthcare, employment, and other areas where racial disparities persist.

The impact of George Floyd's murder extended globally, with people around the world expressing solidarity and joining in the fight against racial injustice. Protests took place in major cities across Europe, Africa, Asia, and beyond, the scope of their reach emphasizing the global nature of the struggle for equality. In the wake of Floyd's murder, legislative efforts were made to address police reform and racial justice. Some states and local governments implemented changes such as banning choke holds, establishing stricter use-of-force policies, and reallocating funds from police budgets to social programs.

I felt a deep sense of responsibility to address the pain and injustice that had been exposed. As a result, my work at DEED took on a new dimension as I expanded my focus beyond workforce development. I channeled my efforts toward the work of implementing public health protections for workers, especially those in essential roles who faced increased risks during the pandemic. My team and I worked tirelessly to create virtual job-training programs specifically tailored to support BIPOC (Black, Indigenous, People of Color) communities, aiming to bridge the opportunity gap and empower individuals who had long been marginalized.

Additionally, Governor Tim Walz and Lt. Governor Peggy Flanagan recognized the importance of rebuilding the small businesses that had been destroyed in the civil unrest following George Floyd's murder. In collaboration with local organizations, community leaders, and volunteers, Minnesota state government provided financial assistance, resources, and guidance to help these businesses get back on their feet. The work was a testament to the resilience of our community and the power of unity in the face of adversity. Every day brought new challenges and emotions.

I visited businesses and saw the broken glass, the impact of looting, and the embers from stores burned to the ground. I cleaned debris and broken glass from a DEED workforce center where people go to find jobs. A little fire damage had occurred, and I made sure the building was boarded up for safety. I joined the hundreds of volunteers who helped clean up the neighborhoods. I helped make sure the voices of young people and activists were heard by the governor.

While visiting with business owners and community residents, I witnessed millions of dollars in property damage, stolen merchandise, and lost income. Business owners told me they hadn't just lost inventory and equipment, they had also lost sleep: on the nights of the unrest and on the nights that followed. When their windows were shattered, their sense of security and peace in the neighborhood was shattered too.

Many of the shops and restaurants that were damaged and destroyed during the unrest were Black-owned, immigrant-owned, or both. Some of them were owned by my relatives. I was determined to be an equity advocate for these workers and businesses.

The weight of the pandemic and the fight for racial justice felt heavier than ever before. But in the midst of it all, I witnessed the incredible strength and compassion of individuals coming together to make a difference. I saw communities rallying around each other, offering support, and refusing to be silenced.

Still, the fight for justice and equality continues. George Floyd's murder highlighted a deep-seated problem that cannot be solved overnight. It exposed the urgent need for systemic change and stirred a collective commitment to dismantling the structures that perpetuate racial discrimination. The legacy of George Floyd's murder lives on through the ongoing work of activists, organizations, and communities fighting for racial justice. His death serves as a tragic reminder of the countless lives lost to police violence and systemic racism and acts as a call to action to create a more just and equitable society for all.

Responding to George Floyd's murder during the pandemic was a pivotal moment in my career and in my personal journey. That event reminded me of the urgent need for systemic change and the profound impact that one tragic event can have on an entire society. It reinforced my commitment to fighting for justice, equity, and inclusivity in all aspects of my work. As I reflect on those challenging times, I am filled with hope for a better future: an inclusive future. The work we and countless others did for Minnesotans was just the beginning. That work was a testament to what communities can do if they refuse to let their differences define them. That is the conviction I hope to pass to anyone who leads a team: inclusion will heal many of your problems. Try it and see.

CREATE AND NURTURE INCLUSION

In our multicultural, multilingual society, organizations can run operations that span different continents and work with people from different cultures. In such circumstances, inclusive leadership, which draws from the strengths and experiences of different cultures, becomes a critical aspect of contemporary team leadership.

Tom Friedman, a *New York Times* columnist and mentor to me, defined this concept in his 2005 best-selling book, *The World Is Flat*. What Friedman means by *flat* is that the playing field of competition between companies from any part of the world is leveling out, and both large and small companies can take advantage of the new connections that are linking the world. Friedman writes that "in a flat world, global corporations will adapt to make the most of global opportunities and global resources—and that increasingly means adapting themselves to a flat world." As companies become nimbler, leaders need to become so too.

With the rise of remote and virtual work arrangements, contemporary team leaders must become adept at leading and managing geographically dispersed teams. In this sense, technology should transcend its role as an enabler of production to also become a tool for strengthening the team spirit. Team members should use technology to communicate better, engage constructively, and boost inclusion.

During the COVID-19 lockdown period in 2021, I saw just how important good team leadership can be to ensuring the well-being of team members. As the deputy commissioner of DEED in Minnesota, I held most official meetings online, as everyone was working independently, in isolation.

When we started the process of assessing what the local communities needed and how the state government could help, our online sessions began in a formal fashion and then gravitated, naturally, toward finding solutions to individual problems related to the loss of lives and livelihoods. I hadn't realized that there were so many people of different racial and cultural origins longing for a chance to open up about their lives and experiences. I am not a psychotherapist, and I didn't know how I would handle the myriad problems that the team members were beginning to share in the forums. At first, this held me back from letting our discussions move in this direction. But how long could I maintain the floodgates before the deluge overran me?

In one of the sessions that I held with a team of young people who had just lost their jobs, a twenty-eight-year-old Italian immigrant revealed how much she longed for the weekly meetings.

"Meeting with you people makes me feel like I belong to this world," she said. "I might not have a job for now, and my family might be thousands of miles away in Italy. I talk to my parents every day, and I have enough food in the house. But I always crave this sense of connection that I get whenever we talk about our shared challenges and how we are going to solve them."

When team members spoke out openly about their experiences, I realized that everyone was willing to help where they could, their personal circumstances notwithstanding. Strangely, talking about this did not derail us from pursuing our collective objective of strengthening livelihood support systems. The cohesion among team members improved, and everyone felt understood and valued.

Indeed, teamwork is guided by clear sets of objectives. For this reason, transformational team leaders need to focus on achieving results, and they must hold themselves and their team members accountable for performance. They should set clear goals, establish key performance indicators, and monitor progress toward objectives. As a way of promoting continuous improvement, leaders need to provide regular feedback to team members, recognize achievements, and address performance issues constructively.

Often, we leaders fear that inclusion may drive us away from these objectives. We worry that if everyone has a voice, then the voice of the team will be lost. But I have found that this is hardly ever the case. If everyone has a voice, the voice of the team is louder and stronger.

Human and intellectual capital in an organization's workforce has become a key source of competitive advantage in modern organizations. To make the most of these crucial assets, the team leader should provide the necessary resources, support risk-taking, and create room for diverse perspectives.

EMBRACE AN ALWAYS-CHANGING, IMPACTFUL TEAM

Consider the following sentence: *We are all in this together!* These words provide us with a simple way to understand the concept of inclusive leadership. Inclusion is the outcome that's reached when empathetic relationships, rooted in respect for human dignity, are activated toward a common goal.

My work on President Biden's Summit for Democracy was an example of inclusive leadership in action. It brought together democratic nations, non-governmental organizations, and common people around the world to advocate with one another for the values of democracy. My life's work to advance racial justice, especially following the murder of George Floyd, was another example of inclusive leadership. Through that work, I brought together local organizations, community leaders, and volunteers to dismantle structures that perpetuate racial discrimination. My leadership response to the COVID-19 pandemic provided yet another example of inclusive leadership, in which technology solutions were implemented so that over 1,400 employees in our department were able to work remotely while also attending to their physical and psychological well-being.

If you want to be an inclusive leader, be clear about the outcomes that you seek. Inclusive leadership is not about being nice to people; it's about achieving impactful results from your team. One of the key ideas in inclusive leadership is the expectation of change. During an important project, the goals might change, your team might change, and you might change. Inclusive leadership is not static, and diversity is crucial. That's because only teams that are open to new ideas can thrive in the face of change.

As an inclusive leader, you need to regularly revisit the goals of your team and the norms of your teamwork. In reviewing these goals and norms, you open your team up to continual improvement. You allow yourself and your team members to learn and grow. You will also want to pay close attention to those who are on the margins of your team: the new members, the departing members, and the temporary members. Inviting them to give their input is often the best way to enable them to honestly share fresh insights about the team and the team's goals. These perspectives may not be easy to hear, but if you are to continue to develop as an inclusive leader, you have to spend some time outside your team's comfort zone.

Here are a few guidelines for ensuring that your leadership is always inclusive:

1. Stay nimble.

Since teamwork is dynamic—with deliverables, timelines, and resources that could change over time—team members should be open to changes and able to handle unforeseen challenges. Each member should be aware of their strategies and demonstrate the willingness to adjust them as needed. This ensures that the team can navigate evolving circumstances effectively.

Being nimble helps a team when new challenges arise, but that's not the only benefit. Nimbleness also enables individuals to take advantage of uncertainty. Opportunities often arise in new markets and underserved populations, and inclusive teams are less afraid of welcoming new people and new ideas.

Another feature of a nimble team is the ability to welcome new members and to celebrate departing ones. Change of team membership can be difficult for a successful team. People build habits of relying on each other, and they build personal friendships around work commitments. Nimble teams cannot be overly reliant on one member or even the leader. They need to be able to celebrate and mourn change while continuing to do the work.

Team members should possess active listening and strong communication skills, to promote easier collaboration, coordination, and understanding. They should also have a track record of working well in teams and possess strong interpersonal skills. Good team members should be able to discuss issues, collaborate, build relationships, and resolve conflicts constructively. They should be reliable, supportive, and able to contribute to a positive team dynamic.

Finally, teams require good leadership to be effective. Assign clear roles and responsibilities within the team. Consider appointing a team leader or project manager who can provide guidance, facilitate collaboration, and ensure accountability. Define leadership roles based on individuals' strengths and expertise.

2. Discourage groupthink.

As a general rule, make sure that your team hires from a diverse pool of candidates. That way, you get a broad range of ideas and perspectives, promoting innovation. Relying solely on the idea of team fit during recruitment—that is, seeking to hire someone similar to other people already on a team—may result in hiring individuals who think similarly to the existing team members. Go a step further and regularly break up cliques that may have fallen into the trap of groupthink. If this pattern is not disrupted, their habitual ways of working may limit the emergence of innovation and fresh perspectives.

3. Encourage collaboration.

An inclusive team not only encourages members to make bold suggestions and challenge each other productively, it also fosters servant behavior. This means that team members work collaboratively on behalf of their colleagues, regardless of who initially proposed an idea. The focus should be not on individual competition but on achieving success as a team.

4. Show solidarity.

Solidarity goes beyond seeking fairness for oneself and involves being an ally and advocate for those who are different. As a leader, you can demonstrate solidarity in a number of ways, such as by advocating for minority employees to receive promotions or raises, addressing your unconscious biases, fighting for improved benefits like paid paternal leave, and dealing with microaggressions. You should not only acknowledge the disadvantages faced by minorities in the workplace but also champion their cause. By leveraging your authority, you can advocate for your team members and strive to secure for them what they deserve.

Being in solidarity with your team members also allows a leader to celebrate individual and collective achievements. Good work should not go unnoticed, and an inclusive leader tries to respond to teammates in ways that are significant to them. Some team members like personal congratulations shared privately, and some would rather be acknowledged publicly in front of a large group. The more significant the achievement, the more thoughtfully leadership should consider how to celebrate individuals and the team.

Conclusion: Inclusive Leadership

In situations where leaders are responsible to a team, inclusive leadership is all about creating a sense of belonging. Inclusive leaders build mutual trust within the pursuit of a common goal. Leaders must listen to team members, normalize the process of continued improvement, and advocate with each member to elicit the necessary support of their contributions. When leaders exhibit such behavior, teams come together. Team members know that they are valued and respected and that they play a part in making a difference. The outcome can be transformative for organizations and for leaders that rely on teams to work together cohesively while simultaneously bringing out the best abilities of each unique member.

PART III

LEADING THE ORGANIZATION

Today's organizations operate in an increasingly globalized and diverse environment. The Internet of Things (IoT)—a phrase that Wikipedia says "describes devices with sensors, processing ability, software and other technologies that connect and exchange data with other devices and systems over the internet or other communications networks"—has made it possible for organizations to have teams distributed across the globe. Teleconferencing and the ability to work remotely have also helped to make this possible. This means that a company could be headquartered in California, employ a global team of the best software developers in India, have production facilities in China, and host customer support services in a business processing center in Kenya. In this way, organizations can recruit and operate with the best global teams at a fraction of what centralized operations would cost. This means that today's organizational leaders must be adept at managing diverse teams, understanding cultural nuances, and fostering inclusion.

Embracing cultural intelligence and creating a work environment that values and capitalizes on diversity are the new currencies that are driving creativity, innovation, and productivity. But does this mean that the right talent is out there just waiting to be picked? Certainly not! With the changing nature of work and evolving skill requirements, leaders face the challenge of attracting, developing, and retaining top talent. Effective talent management and succession planning are critical for organizational continuity and long-term success. Modern leaders must, therefore, headhunt high performers across the globe, provide them with growth opportunities, and create a robust pipeline of future leaders.

I love the following quote from the speech that Steve Jobs, then CEO of Apple, delivered at Stanford University's commencement ceremony in 2005:

You've got to find what you love. And that is as true for your work as it is for your lovers. Your work is going to fill a large part of your life, and the only way to be truly satisfied is to do what you believe is great work. And the only way to do great work is to love what you do. If you haven't found it yet, keep looking. Don't settle. As with all matters of the heart, you'll know when you find it. And, like any great relationship, it just gets better and better as the years roll on. So keep looking until you find it. Don't settle.

Organizational leaders must remain conscious of the changes happening around them and effectively navigate their organizations through transformational initiatives. This requires thoughtful decision-making, effective communication, and the ability to remain calm and to inspire confidence amid uncertainty. Leaders must thus have crisis management strategies in place and be adaptable to rapidly changing circumstances. And of course, they need a strong connection to their ethics in this era of increased transparency and social responsibility. Leaders today are expected to demonstrate integrity, authenticity, and ethical decision-making. They must navigate ethical dilemmas, prioritize the well-being of stakeholders, and establish a culture of trust and ethical behavior throughout the organization. These are the things I will discuss in this section of the book.

At the height of the 2008 economic crash, I was recruited by the Alliance Healthcare Foundation as a senior program officer. The Alliance Healthcare Foundation is the largest independent healthcare foundation in San Diego, with a mission to improve access to healthcare in underserved communities. I served as an ambassador and a bridge between the healthcare efforts of the foundation and the communities impacted by this funding. Through my job at the foundation, we helped tens of thousands of people access health and social services programs. I managed grants to nonprofit groups serving poor San Diegans of all ethnicities, for a total of more than $2.5 million distributed annually. Through these grants, we improved access to healthcare for underserved communities, including refugees and immigrants.

In a 2021 article posted on their website, the U.S. government's National Institute of Health (NIH) identifies cultural respect as a critical concept in the work of reducing disparities in healthcare. Culture is defined as a body of knowledge, belief, or behavior that is specific to groups of people by ethnicity, race, religion, geography, or society. Elements of culture include "personal identification, language, thoughts, communications, actions, customs, beliefs, values, and institutions." The NIH states that culture should be considered when providing healthcare or health information, and they write, "Cultural respect ... helps improve access to high-quality health care that is respectful of and responsive to the needs of diverse patients."

On behalf of the Alliance Healthcare Foundation, I managed the San Diego HIV Funding Collaborative: an organization dedicated to raising and allocating funds for the purpose of reducing the impact of HIV in the San Diego area. To find a more culturally competent home for the collaborative, which originally had been housed at the Alliance Health-care Foundation, I helped lead a yearlong process aided by an advisory committee of donors and concerned community members. The goal was to use funding to strengthen partnerships serving the needs of the HIV/AIDS community in the San Diego region. This search process was open and deliberative, and resulted in the Human Dignity Foundation becoming the new host for the San Diego HIV Funding Collaborative.

Hallmarks of the Human Dignity Foundation include the grassroots nature of its establishment, its history of growth, and its trust-based relationship with its core constituencies, elements that were a good fit for the collaborative. The Human Dignity Foundation was also well suited to advocate for and fund culturally competent healthcare strategies, and it was already helping to educate the broader San Diego community about the fact that HIV/AIDS remains a serious public health issue.

For the sake of clarity, we will define an organization as a group of people who come together to achieve a common goal or objective. An organization is a structured and coordinated entity that comprises people, resources, systems, and procedures that work together to achieve a shared purpose. There are different types of organizations. Commercial enterprises, such as Tesla and Microsoft, exist to make profits and grow their shareholders' wealth, while government agencies, such as the Department of Motor Vehicles (DMV), exist to serve the common good of the citizens. Nonprofit organizations, such as World Vision, cater to the needs of underserved populations, while educational institutions, such as Harvard University, exist to create and disseminate knowledge.

One researcher defines organizational leadership as a management approach in which leaders help set strategic goals for the organization while motivating individuals within the group to successfully carry out assignments in service to those goals. Thus, organizational leadership can be perceived as the ability of leaders to guide, influence, and inspire others to achieve common goals and drive the organization forward.

Since organizations operate in different internal and external environments, transformational leadership would involve setting a clear vision, establishing goals, making informed decisions, and effectively managing resources and people in ways that are specific to the organization. Such leadership helps organizations to navigate through challenges and take advantage of opportunities emerging within their spheres of interest.

Most organizations have well-established structures with clear roles, responsibilities, and reporting relationships that create opportunities for the exercise of both organizational and team leadership. These structures vary depending on factors such as organizational goals, size of the organization, industry, and leadership philosophy, and they determine how tasks are divided, how decisions are made, and how information flows within the organization.

Regardless of which kind of structure you exist in, you can transform your leadership using three principles described in this third section of the book: build on your diverse assets, collaborate to innovate, and accelerate prosperity. Transformational organizational leadership inspires and motivates management and employees to achieve high levels of performance and personal growth. Such leadership is based on a clear vision for the organization and a commitment to creating positive change. While most people look for transformational leadership at the highest management levels, the truth is that this kind of leadership can be implemented at the divisional or departmental level, at the team level, and by individuals.

Transformational leadership can have a profound impact on employee engagement, performance, and organizational success. By inspiring and empowering their followers, transformational leaders create a positive and motivating work environment, drive innovation, and achieve exceptional results. In contemporary corporate America, many transformational leaders have helped their organizations achieve historical feats.

Assets

A GLOBAL VIEW OF HUMAN CAPITAL WITH AMBASSADOR JOHNNIE CARSON

I remember how the morning sun gently peeked through the curtains, casting a warm glow across the room as I stirred awake. It was an important day: I was finally going to attend a meeting that had been marked on my calendar for weeks. As I stretched and yawned, a mix of excitement and nervous anticipation coursed through my veins. With a sense of purpose, I swung my legs over the edge of the bed and let my feet find their place on the cool floor as I began my morning routine. The rhythmic ticking of the clock on the wall reminded me that time was of the essence. I couldn't afford to dawdle. I was meeting Ambassador Johnnie Carson, the newly appointed leader of the U.S.-Africa Leaders Summit Implementation. When given the opportunity, I had known immediately that meeting with the ambassador—someone deeply passionate about African affairs and the role of the African diaspora in shaping foreign policy—was one I couldn't pass up.

As I entered the U.S. Institute of Peace's office in Washington, DC, where Ambassador Carson is based, I was greeted by the ambassador's warm smile and firm handshake. He exuded an air of experience that immediately put me at ease. We settled into a comfortable conversation, discussing the significance of the African diaspora in advancing U.S. foreign policy.

I shared my personal story with the ambassador, recounting the tumultuous years when I was displaced by Somalia's civil war. Growing up in Mogadishu, I had witnessed firsthand the devastating consequences of the war that tore families apart, including my own, and forced us to flee our homes in search of safety and stability. With a heavy heart, I described the hardships we'd endured as refugees, the uncertainty that had clouded our future, and the resilience that kept us going. I explained how, despite the challenges, my journey had eventually led me to the United States, where I found a new home and a strong sense of purpose in advocating for the rights and interests of the African diaspora.

Ambassador Carson listened attentively, his gaze reflecting a deep understanding of the complexities of displacement and its lasting effects. He acknowledged the struggles faced by countless others like me and expressed his commitment to creating meaningful change through engagement with the African diaspora. His career includes ambassadorships to Kenya (1999–2003), Zimbabwe (1995–1997), and Uganda (1991–1994), as well as the role of U.S. Assistant Secretary of State for African Affairs (2009–2013).

I remember how, with a sense of purpose, Ambassador Carson shared the Biden administration's vision of leveraging the immense potential of the African diaspora in advancing U.S. foreign policy in Africa. He spoke of its unique perspectives, connections, and invaluable contributions to the growth and development of both the African continent and America. Together, we brainstormed ideas on how to bridge the gap between the African diaspora and U.S. policymaking, ensuring that voices of the diaspora are not only heard but actively incorporated into decision-making processes.

The African diaspora in the United States is a source of strength and encompasses African Americans—including descendants of enslaved Africans—and nearly two million African immigrants who have close familial, social, and economic connections to the African continent. African Americans have long been foundational to strengthening United States–Africa relations and to shaping United States foreign policy toward Africa—including by actively advocating on the African continent's behalf, even as they struggled to obtain civil rights in the United States.

Today, the African immigrant community continues to make significant contributions to America's growth and prosperity. Ambassador Carson recognized this. He was building on the diverse strengths available to him in his role as special presidential representative for the U.S.-Africa Leaders Summit Implementation. The diaspora represents an enormous foreign policy asset for the United States. No one knows Africa better, or is more connected, than those who have recently come from there, than those who have their heritage there.

SEEING MY SISTER FARDOWSA'S STRENGTHS

The United States is often hailed as the land of opportunity and has long been a beacon of hope for countless people seeking a better life. Among this group, the diaspora community stands strong: a vibrant tapestry woven by diverse cultures, languages, and traditions. But behind the outward beauty of this cultural mosaic lies a narrative of challenges, resilience, and the pursuit of identity. From navigating the complexities of integration to combating stereotypes and discrimination, the diaspora community faces a unique set of obstacles on their journey to embracing their heritage while forging a place in American society.

One of immigrants' biggest strengths is achieved through the navigation of cultural identities. We develop that strength in striking the balance between preserving our cultural heritage and integrating into American society. We immigrants and our descendants navigate the desire to maintain a connection to our roots while adapting to a new culture. Language barriers, generational gaps, and conflicting societal expectations often create an internal struggle, leaving people torn between their ancestral traditions and the pressure to conform. But this journey of self-discovery also results in the development of strength found through introspection, and in a deep sense of cultural pride. I can think of many stories in my personal life that embody this strength, but one stands out. It was the day my sister Fardowsa decided to get her ID.

On this day, she asked me to accompany her to the DMV so she could apply for state identification. In Fardowsa's mind, she was acting responsibly and proactively. She chose to act rather than wait for someone to take her there. She decided we would take a bus to our destination. Fardowsa believed that her communication skills were sufficient to get us to the DMV. I was a teenager so I didn't need an ID. We didn't inform anyone what our plans were or where we intended to go. The DMV was not far from where we lived, but how could we know this without consulting with anyone? We acted in faith.

Fardowsa and I innocently thought that the bus would automatically stop and our destination would be announced when we arrived at the DMV. But this did not happen. Instead, we rode the bus for over an hour. Finally, it came to a halt and the driver announced that the bus had gotten to its last stop. The bus was now heading to a different part of the city. All other passengers departed, but owing to our confusion, we remained seated. This was a new situation for us, and I am not quite sure whether our confusion resulted because of our youth or because we were in a new land with new practices.

Whatever the case, the driver must have sensed our tension because he came up to us and addressed us.

"Folks, we are at our final destination." It was a strange thing to be addressed as *folks*.

Fardowsa, in her broken English, replied, "But where is our place?"

"What do you mean by 'our place,' madam?" asked the driver.

"We need to go to the government building," replied Fardowsa.

"Which government building? I don't seem to understand you."

"Where are we now?" I inquired.

The driver pointed to a map on the side wall of the bus. "This is Aurora. If you are looking for directions, use this map."

We didn't have the slightest idea of how to use the map. In a panic, and worrying about what to do next, we disembarked from the bus. We approached a bystander. He looked middle-aged and was dressed in a long dark jacket.

"We are looking for the government building to pay for the government ID," said Fardowsa.

Looking at us strangely, the man said, "Sorry, I can't help you."

We approached a young lady, but she evaded us even before we had the chance to introduce ourselves. It then dawned on us that we looked different from everyone else. Here we were: me, wearing an oversized suit donated to me by the Church World Service; Fardowsa, wearing her hijab. This was not the kind of clothing appropriate for winter. It was obvious to everyone that we were newcomers to America.

After several unsuccessful attempts at finding out where we were or where we could get help, we finally encountered a man who was kind enough to hear us out. After we'd explained our predicament to him, he said, "I don't understand what you mean by government ID, but if you're looking for a photo center, there is a place two blocks from here." He directed us to the photo shop.

When we got there, Fardowsa said, "We need a government picture."

The young lady behind the counter scanned us from top to bottom. "Sorry, we don't issue IDs here. You will have to go to the DMV."

Feeling a bit relieved and closer to a solution, Fardowsa asked, "Where is that?"

The woman directed us to take a bus that was heading in the direction opposite from where we had come from. We took her instructions and finally found our way to Denver's DMV. Fardowsa filled out the forms and, voilà! We had made an achievement despite the hiccup!

Upon getting Fardowsa's ID, we walked out of the offices and saw a man who resembled us. We guessed he was either Ethiopian or Somali. We approached him and he confirmed he was Ethiopian. His name was Negasi. We then explained our situation to him (speaking in Amharic, an official language in Ethiopia) and told him what we had gone through. We told him that now that we had gotten what we had come for, we didn't know which way was home.

Negasi was so helpful. He seemed to understand our problem perfectly, and he was kind enough to ride with us on the bus and then help us change to another bus that would take us home. After a more than twelve-hour ordeal, we returned home late in the evening. Fardowsa had her "new identity," and I had received an education regarding my sister's persistence. We were strangers in a new land, but she had found the strength to accomplish her goal.

Fardowsa's story is just one example of the way refugees tap into their inner strength. They act, make mistakes, and learn. If my sister had waited, she would not have had an ID. New refugees know the value of action. They have to, because simple things take a long time to accomplish. My sister and I had relied on the kindness of strangers, but we had also asked for help. Taking action and asking for help are strengths to be celebrated.

All of this happens against a background of economic and socio-political barriers. Many people in the diaspora community in the West can tell you a story of discrimination in employment, limited access to quality education, or systemic biases that hinder their ability to fully contribute to society. Overcoming these obstacles often requires perseverance, resilience, and advocacy for equal opportunities. The systems are many times unjust, and individuals can be unfair, and leaders must advocate for justice and fairness. Still, it is important to value the strength that is built through this daily endurance. This strength was present in my conversation with Ambassador Carson. This strength was present in the Biden administration's U.S.-Africa Leaders Summit and in its commitments to strengthen relations with Africa and the African diaspora community. This strength is in my brothers and sisters; it is a diamond in the rough.

PEER REVIEW TO ACCESS ASSETS

Tom Rath is an American consultant on the topics of employee engagement, strengths, and well-being, as well as a best-selling author. He is widely credited with offering the following insight: "You cannot be anything you want to be—but you can be a whole lot more of who you already are." This wisdom challenges the conventional belief that focusing on weaknesses is the key to success. Recent research suggests that prioritizing strengths, rather than first fixing deficiencies, leads to better outcomes for individuals, teams, and organizations. Empowering and successful cultures are built by engaging employees and harnessing their unique capabilities.

When I consider the essence of being truly a transformational leader, different thoughts immediately spring to mind. Not everyone possesses the inherent traits and capabilities required to thrive in such an organizational leadership role. Thus, the question arises: What precisely are the indispensable skills deemed vital for a leader to excel while leading an organization? I suggest that if you want to be this kind of leader, you need to take advantage of your strengths and leverage them for success.

I always had a strong sense of self-awareness: an unwavering belief in my abilities and strengths. For a big part of my career, I navigated challenging situations with confidence, relying on my instincts and knowledge to make informed decisions. Yet there was a part of me that wondered if my self-perception aligned with the reality perceived by others. That doubt was put to rest when I experienced a transformative moment through the power of peer review while I was working for DEED.

As a leader, I understood the significance of feedback, both positive and constructive. I valued the input of my team members, recognizing that their perspectives held tremendous value in shaping our collective success. It was during a performance review session with my direct reports that I received an unexpected gift: an affirmation of the strengths I had always known within myself. Gathered around a conference table, we engaged in an open and honest discussion about our work dynamics, challenges faced, and areas for improvement. As the conversation progressed, my team members began expressing their thoughts and observations regarding my leadership style.

One by one, they shared stories and anecdotes, highlighting instances where my strengths had shone through. They spoke of my ability to inspire and motivate, my keen strategic thinking, and my unwavering dedication to our shared goals. Their words resonated deeply within me, validating the very essence of my leadership approach. They applauded my relationship-building skills, saying things like "Hamse is endearing to those he comes into contact with and is an excellent listener," and "He is willing to go out into the community consistently to get feedback from key stakeholders and has already improved the reputation of DEED enormously since he joined." Some spoke of my presence, passion, political strategy, and creativity. Others loved the depth of knowledge I brought to the team.

Listening to their perspectives, I realized that the impact I had hoped to make as a leader was being felt by those around me. Their feedback went beyond mere compliments; it provided me with a profound sense of validation, confirming that my self-assessment had not been in vain. It was an enlightening moment: a powerful realization that the qualities I valued in myself were truly making a difference in the lives of others.

To be fair, the peer review also offered invaluable insights into areas where I could further develop and enhance my leadership skills. Constructive criticism was delivered with care and respect, highlighting opportunities for growth and providing a roadmap for personal improvement. I embraced their suggestions, and I am eager to continue evolving as a leader and honing my abilities, but now I do so grounded in the truth that my strengths will not steer me wrong.

Armed with the knowledge that my strengths were recognized and valued by my direct reports, I continue to lead with confidence and humility. I know that my journey as a leader is a continuous one, fueled by the feedback and support of those around me. Together, we navigate the ever-changing landscape of our work, knowing that our collective strengths will guide us toward even greater heights of success.

COMING TOGETHER FOR STRENGTHS IN THE AFRICAN DIASPORA

In a thought-provoking article published by CNBC, the author, motivational speaker, and management consultant Marcus Buckingham offered three simple steps for achieving organizational success. In the third step, he emphasized the importance of seeking out activities that bring immense satisfaction: the ones that ignite intellectual growth and fulfillment.

Engaging in tasks that align with our strengths feels natural, leading to a sense of accomplishment. Buckingham urged employees to identify their natural tendencies, skills, and advantages, and to cultivate those aspects of themselves. He likened learning to the growth of new buds on an existing branch, implying that to excel and stand out, individuals must embrace and leverage their beautiful and powerful attributes, transforming them into valuable contributions.

In support of this idea, just think about the draining effect that's caused by activities that go against our strengths, even if we excel at them. According to brain science, low energy levels inhibit our capacity to learn from these experiences. This means that focusing on such tasks hinders growth. It is more beneficial to nurture and promote what we excel at. This enables us to maximize our contributions and maintain a sense of fulfillment in our daily work.

By embracing the philosophy of emphasizing strengths, leaders can unlock their true potential and make significant contributions to their teams and organizations. This shift in focus not only leads to increased success but also fosters a sense of purpose and fulfillment in the workplace. When we recognize and cultivate our unique abilities, we empower ourselves to create meaningful change and experience ongoing growth. How do we do this?

In the fall of 2014, at a roundtable of philanthropic organizations, I began to see a new path for my growth in the field of philanthropy. Catherine Gray of the Minneapolis Foundation had convened twelve foundation leaders to discuss how to meet the needs of the Somali community in Minnesota more effectively. I was one of the few Somali people, if not the only Somali person, employed in Minnesota philanthropy at that time and thus was the only Somali person in the room. I was concerned that this collective might make a rash choice to invest in only one Somali leader or organization, and I argued that the group's assessment should build on the strengths of Somali-led, community-based organizations across the state of Minnesota. Here was an opportunity for the group to listen deeply to the Somali community and to invest in the strengths of emerging leaders.

In 2015, I left my comfortable employment at Margaret A. Cargill Philanthropies to launch Tayo Consulting Group (TAYO): a management and leadership consulting firm made up of experts in both human development and poverty solutions. I leveraged TAYO to build my team of problem-solvers to improve, at a systems level, the health, education, economic opportunities, and social protection of the most vulnerable children and their families. Through TAYO, I was still engaged with philanthropy, but as an outside partner and agent of change. I was free to publicly raise my voice and act for a more just, equitable, thriving, and peaceful world. Traditionally, it's always risky to speak up while working inside philanthropy, particularly for leaders of color.

Now, I was taking a different kind of risk: one that was professional and financial. I was investing in my growth, but would anyone join me? The Minneapolis Foundation saw the unique strengths that I brought to this project, and they were the first to invest in a community needs assessment that would help us to better understand the strengths, challenges, and opportunities common to the Somali community in Minnesota.

By February 2016, my team at TAYO had completed seven months of a culturally specific community needs assessment focused on Minnesota's Somali community. The study highlighted the needs of Somali refugee youth, identified through focus groups, surveys, and interviews conducted with youth, teachers, public safety officials, school administrators, parents, community leaders, and other stakeholders. The report moved away from looking at the symptoms of problems and focused on the root causes. The Somali community in Minnesota was segregated and isolated, partly by choice but also by circumstance. This created misunderstandings and adversarial relationships with institutions.

The assessment provided me an opportunity to bring together leaders of Somali-led community-based organizations in order to utilize their proximity to the community, their trusted relationships, and their leadership to address the needs identified by the report. Through

TAYO, I served as a facilitator and helped found an umbrella organization: the Coalition of Somali American Leaders. The coalition cultivated effective leadership, mobilized resources to foster economic and social development to improve the lives of Somali Americans, and facilitated intercultural exchange to increase awareness, understanding, and appreciation of the Somali community. The philanthropic funders followed the lead of the coalition and invested money in building on these emerging leaders' strengths in order to address the community's needs.

Eight years after this local investment in the strengths of the African diaspora, I was present for the creation of the African Diaspora Council, an initiative born out of the African Leaders Summit. The council was established to strengthen the ties between the United States and the diverse African communities living across the country. The president recognized the tremendous contributions of African Americans, including descendants of enslaved Africans, and African immigrants, who have enriched the nation with their talents, culture, and resilience. He recognized that the diaspora community is the living embodiment of the African Union's Sixth Region, a testament to the unity of the global African diaspora.

As I think about the appointed council members, I am impressed by the diverse strengths of this team. The council is chaired by Silvester Beaman, a bishop of the African Methodist Episcopal Church, and includes members from business, education, athletics, and the arts, including Viola Davis, a philanthropist and one of the world's most accomplished actors. The council's mission is clear: to advise the president on strengthening the connections between the U.S. government and the African diaspora. The task is to foster equity and opportunity for our communities and to promote cultural, social, political, and economic ties between African nations, the global African diaspora, and the United States.

The council has continued to highlight the importance of programs like the Young African Leaders Initiative and the International Visitor Leadership Program, which offer educational and professional exchange opportunities between Africa and the United States. These initiatives nurture the next generation of leaders and foster mutual understanding between our regions.

They also increase the involvement of the African diaspora in trade, investment, and development programs relating to Africa, through government initiatives such as Prosper Africa. They aim to create, by leveraging cultural knowledge and economic expertise possessed by the people and governments in the U.S. and in Africa, mutually beneficial partnerships that can drive growth and prosperity on both sides of the Atlantic.

I have seen firsthand how diversity became the U.S.'s greatest strength. Each person brings unique perspectives and experiences to the table, enriching discussions and ensuring that recommendations are comprehensive and inclusive.

I expect that the impact of the African diaspora will ripple through the nation. There will be increased opportunities for African American and African immigrant entrepreneurs, scholars, artists, and activists. The diaspora's strengths, shared with African nations, will foster stronger diplomatic relations, mutual understanding, and strategic partnerships. I expect the council's work to extend beyond borders and oceans, inspiring other countries to create similar platforms to engage with their African diaspora communities. We will likely become part of a global movement, igniting a flame that spreads across continents, illuminating the potential of unity and cooperation. One of the greatest strengths of refugees, immigrants, and American descendants of slaves is that they act as a bridge between the people in African nations and the people of the United States. At least, this is my hope.

BUILD ON YOUR DIVERSE SET OF STRENGTHS

Leading organizations should start with an understanding of your assets. Explore what is special about your leadership and your team members. Human beings are the foundation of organizational success. If you are going to lead, take stock of the excellence and potential of yourself and your team. While it is important to know the weaknesses and threats to your organization, success is built from the positives.

There are countless ways to evaluate strengths. My sister Fardowsa developed a strong self-awareness regarding her courage and per-sistence—assets shared by many immigrants—through her adventure into the unknown. As a manager, I used human resource management tools to provide positive and constructive feedback in conversation with my team, and I welcomed their assessment of leadership. In my community, I developed a survey instrument that helps identify assets in the Somali community in Minnesota, and the community leaders and I leveraged this information to form the Coalition of Somali American Leaders.

As a diplomat, Ambassador Johnnie Carson used his extensive net-work of relationships to identify the unique assets of people in Africa and the complementary assets in the African diaspora, including both the descendants of enslaved Africans and African immigrants. Building on the ambassador's work, the new African Diaspora Council will need to create metrics for measuring what partners can bring to the work of investing in ties between the United States and the diverse African communities living across the country.

An asset-based leader plans their work around what they do well. What work do you do well? Your work plan should center your talents as a positive contribution to your future. Everyone has talent. Don't plan your leadership only around what you want to do. Remember that you have gifts and that you strive to do good work every day. Your culture and community are sources of strengths; make sure to include them.

Once you can celebrate your assets, consider what more you can learn. Invest your time and treasure in building skills that complement your assets. Every leader should have a plan for learning, for trying new things, and for revealing their potential. You might find new assets that surprise you.

Here are a few ways to make sure you leverage your assets as a leader:

1.   Embrace your strengths.

If you have not already begun the journey of self-discovery, do so by seeking input from others who can help you identify your core strengths. Begin conversations with managers, mentors, peers, or career coaches, whichever apply to you. This will provide you with valuable insights into what makes your leadership unique, valuable, and inspiring. You can also use online resources like CliftonStrengths—an assessment tool from the Gallup company—or the Myers-Briggs Type Indicator to name your strengths. The idea is to be able to concentrate your work on those strengths so that you feel a greater sense of fulfillment and make significant progress in your professional growth.

Remember that your identity, your culture, and your family history are all strengths. Some people who—like me—have a complex economic, racial, and religious identity see only barriers to their future success. They get stuck. The barriers I face are real and beyond my control. What I can control is the story I tell about my complex identity. I claim my identity as an asset, as an abundant gift. I turn my status as a disadvantaged minority into a psychological source of strength. I draw upon this strength to be an effective and innovative leader. When I experience barriers, I can be resilient, choosing hope in the face of adversity. At the root of my story are the trauma of war, the daunting years in refugee camps, and the lesson that even in horror and misery, I was able to transform my private world into a beloved place of beauty. Living in the strength of my story requires a solid moral character and a healthy imagination. My story of strength helps me keep the faith that a more equitable, just, and abundant future is achievable.

2. Avoid comparisons and look for inspiration instead.

Rather than comparing yourself to others, approach those who inspire—or even challenge—you with the hope of learning from them. We live in a vast world in which there is so much to learn from each other. Knowing this will allow you to create room to explore facets of yourself you may not even yet realize exist. When you align yourself with people who may initially elicit a sense of competition, you give yourself permission to learn and grow.

Experiencing another's success can help you identify strengths that you possess but may not have noticed in the past. This is a mindset that opens doors to new possibilities and facilitates personal and organizational growth. Finding people who inspire you can lead you to opportunities to invest in developing your strengths. Witnessing another person's success can inspire you to take a class, learn a new skill, or get a degree. You don't need to compete with someone to be motivated by their success.

Deliberate practice involves focused, purposeful, and systematic efforts to improve specific skills or competencies. It goes beyond routine or casual practice and requires setting clear goals, receiving feedback, and pushing one's limits. Leaders committed to building strengths must embrace deliberate practice as a cornerstone of their growth strategy. Commit to periodic self-assessment. Benchmarking growth over time is a crucial aspect of building strengths and achieving mastery in any field. Leaders should regularly evaluate their strengths, weaknesses, and areas for improvement. This self-awareness enables them to make informed decisions about where to focus their efforts and resources.

3. Capitalize on the strengths of others.

One of the greatest assets of working in a team or with coworkers is the diverse array of perspectives, talents, and skills available to accomplish goals. While no one can be an expert in everything, leaders are often surrounded by others who possess the knowledge and expertise they need to excel. Learning from those around you and capitalizing on their strengths not only leads to achieving objectives but also provides an opportunity to build your team. Actively observe and learn from the experiences of others, allowing their expertise to contribute to your progress.

The icing on the proverbial cake is that by working to build on your strengths, you foster a culture of growth and continuous learning, which not only enhances your personal and professional fulfillment but also contributes to the overall success of your team and organization. With a focus on strengths and a collaborative mindset, leaders can forge a path of personal progress and create an environment where everyone can thrive.

Conclusion: Asset-Based Leadership

At its core, asset-based leadership results from an ongoing assessment of being a leader who builds on strengths. Being able to determine the unique assets of individuals and teams is essential to responding to new opportunities as they arise. When leaders exhibit such behavior, they are ready to meet the moment. Over time, this discernment produces benchmarks that document past achievements and help target future growth. This is the outcome that allows organizations and leaders a pathway to profit from investments in assets.

Innovation

A U.S. VICE PRESIDENT
TALKS WITH A REFUGEE'S DAUGHTER

E arlier on, I shared a story about my daughter Samia and her concerns after the 2016 elections regarding whether we would need to move again. In 2018, I had the opportunity to take her, then nine years old, to meet with former U.S. senator, ambassador, and vice president Walter Mondale. It was a moment I had eagerly anticipated, as he had been both a mentor and an inspiration to me throughout my young adult life and as a student of political science.

As we walked into his office, I couldn't help but feel a sense of awe and nostalgia. The walls were adorned with photographs capturing pivotal moments in American history, reminding me of the immense impact he had made during his time in office. Samia, however, was simply excited to meet someone I'd told her was an important person.

Mondale greeted us with a warm smile and extended his hand to shake mine. His kind eyes twinkled behind his glasses as he turned his attention to Samia.

"Well, hello there, young lady," he said. "It's a pleasure to meet you. Your father has spoken so highly of you."

"Thank you," Samia said.

"You like your school?"

She told him she did. When he asked about her interests, she said that she liked reading best.

"Good, that's good," the former vice president said.

I then prompted Samia to tell him what she wanted to be when she grew up. Samia told him she wanted to be a teacher. He told her that was good too, and she said she didn't know which grade she wanted to teach yet.

Mondale then invited us to take a seat, and we settled down comfortably. Over the next hour, he regaled us with tales of his time in public service, his stories highlighting the importance of compassion, integrity, and dedication. Samia listened attentively, her eyes never leaving his face.

Success in politics requires emerging leaders to be innovative in finding new solutions to problems. I could identify with the account of Mondale's rise to leadership. He had grown up in a family with a deep religious faith, and his family had struggled with poverty. Like me, Mondale had graduated from a state university, and early in his career he had been appointed to roles in both the state and federal government. His leadership championed the civil rights of all people, ensuring all students had access to good schools and that people accused of crimes were provided with lawyers to help defend them.

Mondale's words resonated deeply within me as he spoke about the significance of passing on knowledge to the next generation. Thinking about the increasing attacks on refugees in the United States, I asked Mondale about the right ways to react to the fear and violence.

He answered, "You belong here. You are Americans. And you have as much right to shape our country as I do. It's better that we do it together. There is a lot to be done. If people from your background aren't able to influence the way the government acts, then we are all in trouble. This thing will unravel."

Samia nodded, her eyes sparkling with determination. "Thank you, Vice President Mondale. I promise I'll work hard and make a difference, just like you."

As we said our goodbyes and left the office, I felt an overwhelming sense of gratitude and renewed purpose. Witnessing the interaction between my daughter and such an influential figure in U.S. and global history was a reminder of the incredible opportunities life presents us. It was a humbling experience to see my mentor share his wisdom and inspire the next generation.

A GLOBAL INNOVATOR WHO SAVED LIVES

Before we left Mondale's office, Samia had boldly asked him, "Why did America let refugees come to America?"

He had responded, "America is a country of immigrants, and when I was vice president, we had a big issue about whether we were going to continue to be open as a nation."

He shared that the summer of 1979 had been a challenging period for the United States and the Carter-Mondale administration. President Jimmy Carter had to grapple with escalating energy prices and supply uncertainty that summer. After canceling an energy speech, he sought consultations with business leaders at Camp David to address the perceived national malaise. Although Carter's subsequent energy speech was well received, his decision in 1978 to carry out a poorly executed cabinet shake-up contributed to a sense of chaos. All of this was happening against the backdrop of economic crises and international challenges that were yet to fully emerge.

During this time, the issue of Southeast Asian refugees had not captured the public's attention, even though it represented a devastating disaster. Thousands of refugees had been forced to flee Vietnam following America's withdrawal in 1975. They had escaped on small, leaky boats pushed out to sea or endured overcrowded camps and lived in substandard conditions. Some faced violence at the hands of oppressors, while others perished in shark-infested waters as they searched for a safe haven. Initially, America did little to address this global tragedy. Policymakers lacked both the creativity to develop a solution and the political will to implement an American intervention.

However, the involvement of Vice President Mondale changed that outlook. Mondale convinced President Carter that America's human rights policy would lack credibility if no action was taken to address the refugee crisis. With President Carter's support, Vice President Mondale initiated an innovative plan of action. He persuaded the State Department to denounce Vietnam for its inhumane policies. Furthermore, he urged President Carter to deploy the U.S. Navy's Sixth Fleet to rescue the refugees from the dangers of the sea. Mondale also successfully lobbied for additional funds to establish refugee processing centers in Southeast Asia, assist in refugee resettlement, and commit to admitting fourteen thousand refugees to the United States every month.

Mondale next sought a global solution. He led the U.S. delegation to a United Nations Meeting on Refugees and Displaced Persons in South-East Asia, held in Geneva from July 20 to July 21, 1979. During the conference, he worked to persuade other nations to increase the number of refugees they would accept, to expand temporary camps, and to halt the practice of forcing refugees to embark on dangerous sea journeys.

The highlight of the conference came on July 21, when Mondale delivered a truly historic and unforgettable speech. In his address, Mondale emphasized the unimaginable tragedy and misery experienced by the Indo-Chinese refugees. He drew parallels to the international community's failure to save Jews from Nazi atrocities following the Évian Conference in July 1938, where delegates from dozens of countries had gathered to discuss the issue. Vice President Mondale stressed the need to avoid repeating these mistakes and implored the world to take action.

Mondale outlined a comprehensive seven-point program for an international response to the crisis. This program included pressuring Vietnam to end its inhumane policies, urging first asylum countries (that is, countries that had granted asylum to refugees) to continue their response, and encouraging nations to double their resettlement commitments, as the United States had done. Mondale also emphasized the importance of providing more resources to the United Nations High Commissioner for Refugees (an agency dedicated to the support of refugees and displaced people) and relieving pressure on existing camps. He called for assistance in helping poorer nations resettle refugees and urged other nations to contribute ships for the rescue of people at sea, following the U.S.'s lead.

Mondale rallied world leaders of his generation to learn from the past and to work to rectify the mistakes of previous failures to respond effectively to humanitarian crises. He emphasized the moral principles that should guide their actions and called for meaningful and profound international efforts to alleviate the suffering. He urged the world to forge a global solution to what was becoming a worldwide problem. His speech left a lasting impression with the words, "History will not forgive us if we fail. History will not forget us if we succeed."

You see, it was Vice President Mondale's 1979 speech at the United Nations that helped establish the refugee resettlement system that eventually brought me and my family to the U.S.

THE LAUNCH OF WELCOME CORPS: AN INNOVATION FOR REFUGEES

When I arrived in Washington D.C. to work at the State Department with Uzra Zeya—Under Secretary for Civilian Security, Democracy, and Human Rights—I knew that the refugee resettlement program needed to be modernized. Technology had changed, times had changed, but the policy had remained the same: until now.

In January 2023, Welcome Corps was launched: the new modernized refugee resettlement program made possible by a collaboration of the U.S. government, civil society, and the private sector and engaged with directly by the American people. In a story that illustrates the transformative benefit of collaborating to innovate, the U.S.'s resettlement program is now operating better and is well positioned to reflect America's humanitarian leadership. The American people can now sponsor refugees directly for the first time ever!

In recent times, the American people have shown extraordinary generosity and warmth toward Afghan allies, Ukrainians displaced by war, and those fleeing violence and oppression in Venezuela and other countries. The Welcome Corps is designed to build upon this immense goodwill, creating a long-lasting program that allows Americans from communities across the country to privately sponsor refugees from around the world. It is truly the boldest innovation in refugee resettlement seen in four decades.

A four-year-old girl born in a refugee camp in Tanzania was in the first family to benefit from the Welcome Corps, in the summer of 2023. Over twenty years ago, her grandmother had been a refugee to Tanzania from the Democratic Republic of the Congo (DRC). Now three generations of a family—a grandmother, her two daughters, and her two granddaughters—had found a new home in a thriving, diverse rural community in southern Minnesota. Fifteen residents of Worthington,

Minnesota, had come together to form a Private Sponsor Group (PSG) to host this new family in their community. These United States citizens brought together their many skills and community connections to help the new refugees find housing, access education, and make friends. This sponsorship was assisted by the Minneapolis-based international NGO Alight.

Since its inception in 1980, the United States Refugee Admissions Program (USRAP) had primarily partnered with nonprofit resettlement agencies to provide initial assistance to newly arriving refugees. However, the Welcome Corps aims to create new opportunities for everyday Americans to directly engage in refugee resettlement through private sponsorship. This program will run independently and alongside existing avenues for volunteering with resettlement agencies. It is the intention of the Welcome Corps to—by tapping into the generous spirit of American communities—expand the country's capacity to provide a warm welcome to a greater number of refugees.

To drive the success of the Welcome Corps, the Department of State decided to fund a consortium of nonprofit organizations with substantial expertise in welcoming, resettling, and integrating refugees into U.S. communities. Led by the Community Sponsorship Hub, an organization dedicated to the expansion of community sponsorship in the U.S., this consortium included notable organizations such as Church World Service, Integrated Refugee & Immigrant Services (IRIS), the International Refugee Assistance Project, the International Rescue Committee, and Welcome.US. These are to serve as guides, offering expert advice and support to Americans who join the Welcome Corps.

In addition to the forming of the consortium, community organizations and institutions were invited to participate in the Welcome Corps as Private Sponsor Organizations (PSOs). These PSOs are meant to mobilize, support, and oversee private sponsors, further strengthening the network of assistance available to refugees. Notable organizations such as Alight, Every Campus A Refuge, HIAS, Home for Refugees USA, IRIS, the International Rescue Committee, Rainbow Railroad, and WelcomeNST had already stepped forward to act as PSOs. With the generous support of private philanthropists, the consortium will make funds available to additional qualifying PSOs to bolster their efforts. The Department of Health and Human Services is also to continue supporting U.S. states in building necessary infrastructure and outreach capacity to welcome and aid the integration of new refugees into their communities. Imagine that. Imagine how much good it will do!

For me, the launch of the Welcome Corps was momentous for many reasons. I am excited to think that refugees who enter this country now will find better support and will experience more ease integrating into American life than my family and I did. In that sense, the Welcome Corps is a beacon of hope. It also bears testimony to the important role collaboration plays in bringing about innovation and fostering success for organizations.

It is further a reminder to keep being courageous. At a time when so many people are against refugees, the Biden administration is bold to advance global humanitarian leadership on this issue. It is a job that requires courage because it defies the status quo, but it is a job that must be done, and we are the ones to do it.

COLLABORATION FOR INNOVATION

When leaders come together to address issues, they often aim at agreement, but simply reaching a consensus isn't always the most important outcome of collaboration. It's also important to create new ways to measure success in areas like economic development. That's why we have to start by rethinking collaboration.

Collaboration means finding ways to mobilize everyone's creative abilities to generate value for the organization and community. It is more than just working together. To create real change and tackle complex projects, it's necessary to think together and take action in a coordinated way. Traditional strategic planning isn't always the best approach because it doesn't take into account the unique challenges of transforming our economies. What's needed is a framework for achieving results that's collaborative.

You need a framework that is all about guiding open innovation. This starts with thinking together: actively listening to each other, building on each other's ideas, and collaborating to generate new solutions. After that, the framework should provide a structured process for turning ideas into action: setting clear goals, identifying the right people to involve, and defining specific action items to move the project forward.

Collaborative innovation is all about bringing people together to share ideas, knowledge, and resources, in order to solve problems and come up with innovative solutions. It's a process that can deliver real value to an organization. To build a culture of innovation through collaboration, there are many steps and processes to follow. It starts with ensuring that both internal and external stakeholders are on the same page and working together toward common goals. Communication is key in the initial phase, as communication helps people within the organization share objectives and goals for achieving innovation. This approach should then be expanded to include partners and other external stakeholders.

When it comes to internal stakeholders, it's important to recognize their value and involve them in the innovation process. This not only engages and motivates employees but also prepares them to collaborate with external stakeholders. One way to do this is by creating a platform for employees to share their experiences and ideas for improving interactions. Including internal stakeholders in the innovation process helps them to see the impact of their involvement and to make a difference to both the organization and its customers.

Collaborating with external stakeholders such as network organizations and cocreators is equally important and can have tremendous results, as it did with Welcome Corps. When selecting these stakeholders, it's crucial to identify those who have common goals and values with your organization. They should also have the necessary expertise and resources for effective collaboration.

Innovation through collaboration is becoming increasingly important in today's fast-changing and globally competitive market. Businesses realize the need for frequent and high-quality innovation processes. Open approaches and business models are being embraced to address the challenges of rising development costs and shorter product life cycles. Collaborative innovation is the future of business development, and when integrated into an organization's business strategy, it can support digital transformation efforts. Embracing it will unlock your organization's potential for growth and lead to success.

COLLABORATE ON CONCEPTS TO PRODUCE TANGIBLE SOLUTIONS

Innovation is the process of assembling the best ideas and creating space to try new things. Being innovative means bringing the assets of the team together to experiment. Innovation then multiplies the strengths of the team, benefiting the organization and contributing to overall prosperity. I brought my daughter to visit former vice president Walter Mondale, who himself met with innovative policymakers whose solution for refugees in the 1970s paved the way for my family to enter the United States in the 1990s. Mondale demonstrated how global leadership can be innovative, and I built on this with my support of Welcome Corps. The innovation of refugee resettlement will open doors for U.S. citizens to play a more active role in welcoming new Americans. Innovation requires collaboration within which individuals share and test creative solutions.

Innovation is rarely successful at its first attempt. When I arrived in Minnesota, I saw that the Somali community had some of the worst health outcome indicators in the state. In San Diego, I had been a leader of the Alliance Healthcare Foundation, and I now saw what seemed like a good business opportunity. I set up a social enterprise to help the community address the health challenges and to help people within the community get services from one of their own.

I invested my own money and got support from my family, but the demands on my time were more than I anticipated. No one in my family was inspired to run with this dream. None of the potential investors understood the business model. This was a failure, and I regretted that I hadn't done my homework. My innovative idea was over before the business opened its doors to its first clients.

However, with the spirit of innovation, I continued to meet more people and share ideas. For a time, I considered becoming a publisher, drawn by the idea of sharing the lived experiences and aspirations of Black, Indigenous, and People of Color (BIPOC) writers within Minnesota and neighboring states. Noble and timely as the idea of a publishing house was, none of the investors that I talked to chipped in. The content developers and editors, though agreeing on the need, insisted that they weren't keen on joining the venture as partners. I eventually had to let go of the dream, painful and expensive as it, too, had become.

It was only after these two failed attempts at innovation, and countless other failed ideas, that I met the partners who would form BanQu: a financial technology start-up that I will discuss in the next chapter. Innovative leadership is a search for the most beneficial and profitable ideas, and it is dependent on a leader's willingness to experiment, learn, and try again.

An innovative leader brings value to an organization by thoughtful risk-taking: using a creative and entrepreneurial mindset to disrupt the status quo. To be an innovative leader, you need to dedicate time to critical thinking. You can invite your team to brainstorm and help them see new opportunities. You can leverage the resources of the organization, including talents, finances, and time, to focus on being more efficient. You can create a pilot project to test your team's capacity to meet new opportunities. You can seek extra help to complement the strengths of your team. You can prioritize underserved people as untapped markets for organizational growth.

I recommend the following five actions to foster innovation:

1. Listen and explore.

Take the time to actively listen and explore ideas and perspectives from all stakeholders involved in the collaborative process. The point here is to create room for open communication, active engagement, and a deep understanding of the various viewpoints and forms of expertise within the group. By actively listening, you create a space for open dialogue and knowledge sharing. This allows for a better understanding of the challenges, opportunities, and potential solutions related to the specific project or initiative. Actively listening helps build trust, strengthens relationships, and promotes a sense of inclusivity among the participants.

While you're at it, be sure to delve into the different ideas, possibilities, and potential pathways for action. Encourage participants to think beyond the obvious and to consider innovative solutions. The idea is to create a rich and diverse pool of options to address the challenges at hand. Together, listening and exploring set the foundation for the collaborative process. They help to create a sense of shared purpose and commitment among participants, as everyone feels heard and valued, and they foster a collaborative environment where diverse expertise and knowledge can be leveraged for effective decision-making and action planning.

Rely on the diverse strengths of your team members when seeking out new problems to solve and new markets to serve. One of the results of having an inclusive team is that you're able to see differences and possibilities more quickly than if you had a traditional, monolithic team. There can be an economic benefit in being the first to serve a new market or the first to solve an urgent but unseen problem.

2. Learn and adjust.

Learning and adjusting has to do with the iterative process of evaluating progress, learning from successes and failures, and making adjustments to achieve desired outcomes. The idea here is to be committed to continuous improvement and to adapting to new information and changing circumstances. Learning in collaboration involves analyzing the data, feedback, and results from previous actions and projects, so that you can identify key takeaways and insights. This information helps participants understand what worked, what didn't, and what adjustments can be made moving forward to ensure continued progress. Adjustment means modifying plans and strategies to reflect what was learned during the learning phase.

Remember that while collaborating, you want to make sure that teams remain on track, achieve their goals, and meet expectations. Adjustments then can involve reprioritizing tasks, modifying project timelines, reallocating resources, or even pivoting entirely to a new approach. When you learn and adjust, you ensure that the collaborative process remains effective and relevant in the face of changing circumstances or new information. Learning and adjusting allows teams to continually improve their approach, build on previous successes, and take corrective action if needed to ensure that they are achieving their goals.

3. Focus and align.

Here, the idea is to concentrate efforts and resources on the most important areas that align with the general strategic objectives of the collaboration. You will want to set clear priorities, coordinate actions, and make sure everyone is working toward a common goal. To effectively collaborate, you need to identify and prioritize the key areas that will have the greatest impact on achieving the desired outcomes. This involves evaluating different options, considering available resources, and making informed decisions about where to allocate time, energy, and resources. When you focus on the right areas, your teams can optimize their efforts, avoid unnecessary distractions, and achieve meaningful results.

In the same vein, aligning is about making sure that all stakeholders and participants are working in harmony toward a shared purpose. This involves aligning their actions, objectives, and strategies to support the overall goals of the collaborative effort. Aligning requires effective communication, regular coordination, and the establishment of common expectations and standards.

When you focus and align, you make sure that the collaborative effort remains on track and moves forward cohesively. By focusing on the most important areas and aligning their actions, participants maximize their collective impact and increase their chances of achieving their desired outcomes. Additionally, they maintain clarity of purpose and eliminate any potential conflicts or misunderstandings among participants. When everyone is focused and aligned, they are better equipped to collaborate effectively, make informed decisions, and adapt to changing circumstances.

4. Link and leverage.

Whenever collaborating, make sure to connect and leverage resources and relationships in a way that bears strategic advantage. Build connections and partnerships with organizations, individuals, and entities to create synergies and enhance collective impact. This will mean forming strategic alliances, collaborations, and networks to access diverse expertise, share resources, and expand the reach and influence of the collaborative effort. Through linking, participants get to pool their knowledge, skills, and resources, in order to tackle complex problems and pursue shared objectives.

Leveraging, on the other hand, involves maximizing the value and impact of available resources and assets. It involves identifying and utilizing existing strengths, capabilities, and opportunities to achieve greater outcomes. This can include leveraging financial resources, intellectual property, technological capabilities, influence, or other assets that can provide a competitive advantage or accelerate progress.

The goal of linking and leveraging is to amplify the collective impact of the involved organizations and achieve outcomes that would be difficult to attain individually. The process enables participants to access a broader range of expertise, resources, and perspectives, leading to more innovative and effective solutions.

5. Create value.

Genuine innovation requires that you create value. Any organization worth its salt prizes implementing ideas and programs that add value. If you look around, you will see that it is the businesses that have consistently delivered innovative products that meet customer needs that withstand economic downturns. Notably, you could create value through incremental improvements to existing products, the creation of entirely new products and services, or reducing costs. The choice is yours, but you must create value in some way to remain relevant in a constantly changing world.

I have noticed that to minimize the risks of damaging established brands, many companies create experimentation brands, joint ventures, or co-brands to test new ideas and create value. For instance, Toyota's Scion brand was targeted at younger consumers, unlike its mainstay, which was targeted at baby boomers. Toyota used four innovative methods during the process—namely need-finding, framing, creative combination, and prototyping—to ensure that the product delivered value.

Need-finding is about spotting new opportunities, while framing involves searching for patterns to understand customers' experiences better. Creative combination entails bringing together concepts and viewpoints to develop the best options for meeting the customers' needs. Prototyping is a process of rapidly developing ideas worthy of more in-depth study. It enables a quick determination of whether an idea is worth pursuing or discarding and allows for continuous refinement of the idea. As an organization, you can borrow a page from Toyota's book and use any one of these methods while collaborating to create value.

Conclusion: Innovative Leadership

When growth is the goal, innovative leadership is about having unsatisfied optimism and being a leader who collaborates to create value. Collaboration mobilizes the organization's abilities to think together, seek support, set clear goals, and take action in a coordinated way. When leaders exhibit such behavior, they will benefit from success and failure. Through collaboration, leaders generate value from both new solutions and solved problems. All organizations and leaders seek to profit from the new value that serves their mission.

Prosperity

AN ECONOMIC INVESTMENT
FOR NORTH CENTRAL AFRICA

Margaret A. Cargill Philanthropies is the largest philanthropic foundation in Minnesota and one of the largest in the world, with a mission to provide meaningful assistance and support to society, the arts, and the environment. In 2012, I was recruited by the organization to serve as a senior program officer. One of the key priorities that needed to be urgently addressed was the issue of severe hunger in the Sahel region of West Africa.

The Sahel is located between the Sahara desert to the north and the lush coastal regions along the Atlantic Ocean. In that transition between desert and jungle, the land is mainly flat, semiarid grassland. From 2010 to 2014, the Sahel region of West Africa experienced three severe food crises due to poor rains, inflated food prices, and limited pasture for animal grazing. Poor families were forced to sell land or livestock, go into debt, and limit their food consumption just to survive.

In January 2014, we provided a $1.5 million grant to Lutheran World Relief to scale up their successful community-based, resilience-building work in Niger, Mali, and Burkina Faso in West Africa. I admired the fact that, even as there was an immediate crisis in the region, this program took a long-term view and prioritized community recovery and resilience. Immediate humanitarian food assistance was provided, along with education about sustainable agricultural development. The farmers were living in a cycle of low agricultural productivity and low farm incomes, and Lutheran World Relief provided livestock such as goats and sheep, and training on animal care.

The farmers also accessed certified seeds for millet, sorghum, and cowpeas, and training in improved crop production. Some of the grant funding went directly into the hands of farmers, in the form of income from jobs building terraces, trenches, stone walls for soil and water conservation, and warehouses for crop storage. The funding helped more than one hundred thousand farmers in the Sahel region be less vulnerable to future food shortages.

One of the important lessons I learned was that these farmers needed to be meaningfully connected to the global economy. The ability to access information, connect with others, and participate in the global economy has become the gateway to endless opportunities. In this context, empowering the world's poorest to be connected to the global economy is not just important but vital.

Connecting the world's poorest to the global economy opens up doors to economic growth and development. When provided with access to digital technologies, financial services, and e-commerce platforms, individuals living in poverty can tap into new markets and opportunities. They can start businesses, trade goods and services, and participate in global supply chains. This in turn stimulates local economies, creates jobs, and drives income generation, lifting people out of the vicious cycle of poverty.

In addition, access to information is a game-changer in the fight against poverty. When the world's poorest are connected to the internet, they gain access to a wealth of knowledge and educational resources. This enables them to enhance their skills, learn about new technologies, and stay informed about market trends. When the information gap is closed, individuals can make informed decisions, seize entrepreneurial opportunities, and acquire the knowledge needed to succeed in the global economy.

It is also true that empowering the world's poorest to be connected to the global economy promotes inclusive development. When traditionally marginalized communities gain access to digital technologies, they can participate in decision-making processes, access their credit history and health records, voice their concerns, and advocate for their rights. Connectivity also facilitates access to essential services such as healthcare and education, bridging gaps in social and economic inclusion. Through breaking down barriers, connectivity ensures that no one is left behind, creating a more equitable and just society.

I have also found that when disaster strikes or crises emerge, access to information and digital tools becomes a lifeline. Connected communities can receive early warnings, access emergency services, and receive vital assistance. Furthermore, connectivity allows for the quick dissemination of critical information, ensuring that resources are allocated effectively and recovery efforts are accelerated. By empowering the poorest with connectivity, we equip them to withstand and recover from various hardships that may come their way.

MEETING THE FINANCIAL NEEDS OF A WOMAN FARMER

A little over a decade ago, in the heart of Africa, nestled within the verdant landscapes of the Democratic Republic of the Congo (DRC), Ashish

Gadnis began what he didn't know would be a life-altering journey. As the new volunteer for an American Refugee Committee project funded by USAID, he found himself navigating the intricate challenges and vibrant tapestry of this captivating land. Having grown up in Mumbai, in India, Ashish had witnessed firsthand the stark inequality of the world, and from an early age he had started to question it. He had been particularly curious about the caste system, wondering why children of different backgrounds were not allowed to play together.

Ashish had always been driven by a deep sense of purpose: a burning desire to make a positive impact in the lives of those less fortunate and to make right the wrongs of the world. His role in the American Refugee Committee project offered him the opportunity to do just that by overseeing innovative ways to improve healthcare, education, and sustainable development in the Congo. From the moment he arrived, Ashish was enveloped by the rich culture and warmth of the Congolese people. Welcoming smiles greeted him, the people's resilience and infectious spirit becoming his constant companions. However, beneath the surface, he discovered a region marred by conflict, poverty, and social inequality.

Ashish immersed himself in his work, collaborating with local organizations, community leaders, and dedicated volunteers who shared his vision of bringing positive change to Congolese families. Among other initiatives, Ashish organized a project to build a water tower in the eastern DRC. This is work that required him to collaborate with volunteers, mostly unemployed youths, who would erect the structure. He also needed to partner with fundraising volunteers in the U.S. During this period, he noticed a trend: many aid organizations were bringing free stuff to the people of the DRC, but the organizations ended up creating dependency. He says that instead of delivering dignity, the help felt like an act of pity. Ashish was more concerned with providing help that did not take away a person's dignity.

One of the ways he found to ensure dignified help was by involving volunteers in the water project every step of the way. He oversaw the messaging for the campaign. He ensured that the planning involved the volunteers. He sat down with farmers in their homes and told them of the work the volunteers were about to do. He asked questions, hoping to learn all he could. He ate what the locals ate and sat where they sat. He wanted to understand what was meaningful to them rather than simply design a project and leave.

On one fateful morning, his job had him helping a poor woman farmer open a bank account. She was the provider for her family. She worked her small plot of land and grew essential global resources out of the soil. She lived with abuse, inequality, and unsanitary conditions, but even in the face of many tragedies, she had hope.

For years, she'd sold her goods into big brands' supply chains. But now, standing in front of the banker, she had nothing to show for her hard work. He wouldn't accept her paper receipts as proof of a financial history. No one up the supply chain knew her. The local bank used all sorts of ridiculous excuses to deny her.

"I don't know what to tell you." The banker shrugged. He looked at Ashish and said, "I can't bank her." Then he looked Ashish up and down for a moment and added, "I'll bank you." It hit Ashish then: to the bank, he existed and the woman didn't.

The name BanQu comes from this response, "I'll bank you." BanQu means to give women like her the transactional identity that global financial systems need to track, to allow them to build credit history. Without proof of her supply chain participation, that mother would never break the cycle of extreme poverty and gender inequity.

In an online interview with Meaningful Business, an organization whose mission is to help purpose-driven leaders succeed, Ashish wrote, "Millions of the poorest farmers (especially women), waste-pickers, recyclers, artisanal miners, factory workers and refugees slog every day in our global supply chains—making our jeans, mining cobalt for our iPhones, growing coffee for our $10 'fair-trade' latte, picking up our yoghurt cups and plastic bottles but are completely invisible, 'un-bankable' for the simple reason that they cannot prove their existence in global supply chains. . . . This invisibility prevents them from improving their lives."

Ashish and I shared a vision to end inequalities affecting refugees, women farmers, and other underserved, underinvested communities. We decided to create—along with our third cofounder, Jeff Keiser—a revolutionary economic digital identity platform that allows people who are excluded from our global economic ecosystem to gain access to the global economy.

BanQu is the first digital economic identity platform that harnesses the benefit of a distributed ledger. It provides an ID that is linked with critical information such as health data, education records, economic assets, and property records. The platform even provides financial support details from family members overseas, which can be used to demonstrate a stable income.

The BanQu ID, linked with the person's critical information, is completely owned and controlled by the user who creates it. It provides full privacy, and the user gets to decide who to share information with and when. These innovative features are made possible by blockchain technology, which forms the basis of this platform. The blockchain is a ledger or a new type of application that stores permanent data, which can be shared without needing a central administrator. Everyone who participates in a trade on the blockchain gets an equal and secure copy of the transaction. It contrasts dramatically with our traditional databases, which are controlled and owned by one single administrator, and affords users unparalleled security, easy accountability, and guaranteed integrity.

Imagine how different that woman's story would have been if she had had access to a digital ID like the one provided by BanQu. She could have accessed whichever service she needed and transformed her life with it because her data would have been stored in one place.

Now, for the first time ever, she and people like her will be empowered to control their data instead of being at the mercy of other people who control a piece of their information. BanQu allows a person to be part of a network. The person gets to decide who to give access to their information and when to revoke that access. Since the network connects all the data points in one place, the person can build a credit profile and a transaction history.

For us, BanQu is about bringing prosperity to people like the woman Ashish met. It is about doing what is right and giving refugees and other underserved communities a way to get the services everyone else gets easily. It is about rectifying inequality.

Today, BanQu serves over fifty-four countries, in thirteen languages, with over 2.5 million people connected. By all accounts, the platform has prospered. And it continues to, because it is underpinned by an inalienable truth: if you lead your organization from a place of service—if your goal is to do right—then success is just one step away. What's more, that success will be sustainable because your profits do not harm others; rather, they empower them.

VALUE FOR THE INVESTOR

BanQu not only serves the poorest people seeking economic identity, it also serves business clients: the large companies that are buying and sourcing their coffee, cacao, or jeans from people who live in extreme poverty. BanQu allows leading brands to promote responsible sourcing while creating an audit trail of their dealings with the producers of their raw material. As a profit-for-purpose software company, BanQu sells software to these brands who want to make their supply chains transparent, traceable, and—most importantly—equitable. As Ashish said to

Meaningful Business, "If the CEO of a beverage company cannot name one waste-picker on the streets of Lagos, or the CEO of a smartphone company cannot prove that children are in school, or the CEO of a chocolate company cannot name a smallholder mama farmer, then we don't have equitable, traceable, and transparent supply chains."

By tracking goods across the value chain to the source, the system empowers manufacturers to take better care of the environment and account for the goods that reach their end of useful life in responsible ways. Brands can now prove that they are meeting their United Nations sustainable development goals (SDGs) and environmental, social, and governance goals (ESGs).

For BanQu, the wealthy are not only investors and large corporate brands, they are also successful immigrants like Ashish and me, trying to send money to our extended families in extreme poverty settings. Many banks in the United States refuse to transact with financial institutions in some countries due to a lack of a credible identity management system that can satisfy regulatory requirements; the few financial organizations that do offer this service charge high fees. Many businesses and people therefore stash cash in a bag and fly out to countries that have fewer restrictions to conduct the transactions from there. This is a high-risk business, and these barriers to money transfer mean that life-sustaining resources through remittances are delayed or denied to the parents and siblings who depend on this support. By serving these successful immigrants, BanQu can contribute to strengthening families by helping to transfer much-needed money to people in refugee camps and developing countries. It's a sustainable social impact model!

I first learned about social impact from Jerr Boschee. In my role as a senior leader with Alliance Healthcare Foundation, I invited Jerr to keynote the Innovation in Healthcare conference in 2011 in San Diego. He is the former CEO of the National Center for Social Entrepreneurs and a cofounder of the Social Enterprise Alliance. Jerr's social impact crossed the private, nonprofit, and public sectors as he served as a senior executive for a Fortune 100 company, a managing editor for a chain of regional newspapers, a Peace Corps volunteer in India, and a renowned lecturer in higher education.

Jerr provided me with lessons for social impact leadership that I continue to use today. Social impact is about action, not ideas. He shared with me what he referred to as the Noah Principle for social impact, "No more prizes for predicting rain. You only get a prize if you build an ark!" Prosperity is not something to wait for, and problems don't exist to be complained about. Problems exist to be solved. Jerr gave me the following tool for assessing whether an investment is focused on social impact. He said, "If your vision is inner-directed, you're not starting with the people you serve; you're starting with your own ambitions." Social impact investments start with the people.

In our way, my wife and I are social impact investors. In the culture of our families and our faith, it is not customary to talk about charitable giving. Seeking attention diminishes the value of the giving. However, I can say that a significant amount of our income goes to investment in others, including charity. The word *charity* might call to mind the old and the infirm, but our family giving also supports education and business development for large families in Africa. This giving is an investment in these families. Our children sometimes question our giving, and the consequence of giving is that our children do not have all the comforts that some of their peers have. But my wife and I believe that giving back to those in need sustains us, and I hope our children come to value and continue this tradition.

This example of giving is very common in the Somali community. One of the five pillars of Islam is *zakat*: the religious duty of all Muslims with wealth to help the needy. I spoke with a friend who works at a community-owned money transfer company similar to Western Union, and he estimates that Minnesotans send about $50 million a month to

Somalia, Ethiopia, and Kenya. That is just the informal network known as *hawala*. When you include online payments and traditional bank wires, the amount is a lot more! This social giving can be an engine for economic development and growth.

DO THE RIGHT THING AND MAKE PROFITS

If you grew up associating businesspeople with unchecked greed, you might wonder if it's possible to make a profit and still do the right thing. After all, businesses need to charge more than their costs to make money. But does that mean they're taking advantage of customers? And is it too expensive to invest in clean energy, pay fair wages, and support social causes? Well, here's the good news: you can make money and be a responsible corporate citizen.

Corporate social responsibility (CSR) is an approach to managing organizations that includes social and environmental issues in the day-to-day operations of the business and in the business's relationships with external stakeholders. CSR is not only about what companies do with their profits, it is also about how they make profits. It looks at the institutional supply chain for production and it also looks at individuals' ethical conduct within the organization.

While CSR is a broad concept, ESG (environmental, social, and governance) goals articulate a framework with more specific criteria to help stakeholders measure the company's approach to risk and opportunities. CSR is most often defined by a company's internal policies, whereas ESG is often compared to external benchmarks. CSR and ESG initiatives can include adopting clean energy solutions to reduce a company's carbon footprint, being proactive about labor laws and about providing fair benefits to employees, supporting local or global charities, and so forth. Essentially, when I talk about ethical prosperity, I'm referring to paying attention to your environmental, philanthropic, economic, and ethical responsibilities as an organization.

Today, organizations of all shapes, sizes, and locations are embracing doing good: and for good reason. Today's consumers are socially conscious, and this awareness directly influences their purchasing decisions. If an organization doesn't prioritize responsible business practices, customers are less likely to engage with them. Research from PDI Technologies shows that 74 percent of consumers care about the environmental impact of the products they buy, and 68 percent are willing to pay more for sustainable products. And when it comes to younger consumers, the trend is even more prominent: 91 percent of Gen Z respondents say they prefer to buy from sustainable companies.

So, it's clear that being a responsible organization isn't just the right thing to do; it's also a smart business move. By aligning your organization with socially responsible practices, you not only gain the trust and loyalty of consumers, you also tap into a growing market of socially conscious customers who are willing to invest in companies that share their values. My central argument here is that making a profit and doing the right things for society are not mutually exclusive. By considering the environmental, social, and governance impact of your organization, you can not only contribute to the greater good but also reap the benefits of a more sustainable and prosperous future.

ACCELERATE GROWTH TOWARD ETHICAL OUTCOMES

Prosperity is the outcome when people come together with an asset-based approach to innovate solutions that create value. Increased regional prosperity for small farmers was the idea behind Margaret A. Cargill Philanthropies grants to Niger, Mali, and Burkina Faso in West Africa. Increasing prosperity brought my friend, Ashish, to work with the people of Congo to bring clean water to their communities.

Increasing prosperity brought the mama farmer to seek a bank account and led to the creation of BanQu. Increasing prosperity is a reason that leading brands work with BanQu to document the ethical sourcing of their coffee, cacao, or jeans. Families like mine share their income with families in poverty around the world to invest in their education, support their business start-ups, and increase prosperity.

These are examples not only of investments in prosperity; these are also examples of attempts to ethically increase prosperity. As a leader for prosperity, you can be socially conscious about your purchasing decisions. You can bring forward your assets and innovative ideas to work directly with the world's poor toward mutual economic growth in new markets. You can give generously to social needs once your basic needs are met. You can invest your income and your investment returns in ventures that seek both profits and economic justice. You can embrace this wisdom from a college professor and United States senator mentioned earlier in the book, Paul Wellstone, who said, "We all do better when we all do better."

Here are a few ways that you can, as a leader, balance prosperity and impact:

1. Think long-term.

Organizations should always keep sustainability in mind. Whether you're developing new products, services, or initiatives, consider sustainability and appeal to socially conscious consumers. Remember, sustainability is a long-term game. For instance, small businesses don't need to feel overwhelmed by ESGs and worry about immediate financial returns. Instead, start thinking about the long-term benefits. When you consistently demonstrate that you care about sustainability, customers will develop loyalty toward your brand. While ESGs may not have an immediate impact on your financials for the next quarter, they can produce a sustainable return on investment (ROI) in the long run.

2. Address economic injustice.

There are times when the economic system is broken and people must speak out for justice. During the COVID-19 pandemic, I witnessed young people take on the State of Minnesota and win! The pandemic resulted in record-high levels of unemployment, but a 1939 state law prohibited workers still in high school from receiving financial benefits when unemployed. In 2020, many businesses closed and laid off their employees, but high-school-aged workers and their families did not receive unemployment benefits. These young people organized, and with the support of a youth-serving nonprofit, Youthprise, the youth took the State of Minnesota to court.

They also shared their stories with government officials. In my service as the head of Workforce Development for DEED, I was moved by their stories of economic hardship and increased stress. On December 1, 2020, the courts ruled in favor of the young people, and they could now collect unemployment benefits. The economy works better, and people are more prosperous, when they organize for economic justice.

3. Give to others.

Are you a sharer or a hoarder? If you are blessed to have more than you need, you are prosperous. Ethical traditions across the world share the value that says people have a duty to improve the lives of others. You can give as a volunteer, as a friend, and as a financial benefactor, and you can receive the joy of giving. Though philanthropy alone cannot solve all the world's problems, the gifts of your time, talent, and treasure can make a difference.

4. Enjoy your life.

The writer Kurt Vonnegut wrote a poem titled "Joe Heller" that's about prosperity and the dangers of being a hoarder. His words focus on the blessing of abundance. In the poem, Vonnegut asks Heller how he feels about the fact that their billionaire host possibly made more money in a day than Heller's novel *Catch-22* had made in its lifetime. Heller answers that he has something the billionaire doesn't: the knowledge that he has enough.

Being ethically prosperous includes having fun! Take time with friends and family. Take time to be with yourself. The purpose of prosperity is to delight in abundance. While there are times in life that require the temporary sacrifice of enjoyment—maybe when you're starting a new business, for example, or getting an education—your goals should result in a life you love.

Conclusion: Leadership for Prosperity

Leadership for prosperity is about being a leader who accelerates growth toward ethical outcomes. When investing their resources, leaders prioritize opportunities where the profit contributes to emerging businesses, health, and the environment. When leaders for prosperity exhibit such behavior, they choose abundance. As a result of solving problems, prosperous leaders make profits while they grow local economies, advance global trade, and support people rising out of poverty. Making a profit while doing the right things for society is an outcome desired by ethical organizations and leaders.

PART IV

Leading
the Community

Community is about groups of people, and communities can be defined by geography, culture, beliefs, familial relationships, shared interests, and common practices. A community also requires awareness of a unique identity as a group. Community is a social unit where individuals come together to form connections and relationships, and to build a sense of belonging. The definition of community can be broadened to include factors like location (for example, a neighborhood), shared interests (such as soccer), and sociocultural factors (such as Indian American identity). Communities can even be virtual in nature. The American author, educator, and activist Parker J. Palmer is credited with defining community emotionally as "a place where the connections felt in our hearts make themselves known in the bonds between people."

Boulder, Colorado, for instance, is known for its vibrant community and high quality of life. It has a strong inclination toward environmental sustainability, great outdoor recreation facilities, and a thriving arts scene. The city is also known for its diverse start-up ecosystem in renewable energy, outdoor sports, and natural foods. Another good example of a community would be Eastleigh: a neighborhood in Nairobi, Kenya, that is globally renowned as a hub for business. The community attracts some of the brightest business minds and has supported the growth of many successful malls and industries.

In contemporary America, community needs vary widely, depending on a myriad of factors such as geographic location, demographics, socioeconomic conditions, cultural diversity, and historical context. The needs and challenges faced by individuals within any neighborhood, or within any racial or ethnic community, are diverse. For this reason, the effectiveness of community leaders is judged by the leadership's success in identifying, articulating, and mobilizing solutions to the needs of the communities they lead.

So, in this book, when I refer to community leaders, I mean people widely perceived as representing a community. The leader is seen as a vision carrier, influencer, mobilizer, and reliable guide who leads the community toward improving their welfare and solving societal problems. A transformational community leader creates impact by inspiring and mobilizing individuals toward positive change. These leaders are self-aware. They understand that successful community leadership begins with good personal leadership. It also starts with an appreciation of one's strengths and weaknesses, and a desire for continuous personal development. The leaders also understand the limits of their thoughts and ideas, recognizing that there are multiple perspectives to an issue, and that they must therefore consult their people and value others' ideas.

These leaders are also visionaries. Transformational community leaders engage in collaborative dialogue to understand the needs and aspirations of the community, and to develop a shared vision for its future. They then create and articulate their visions for a better community and motivate community members to pursue the same and help their communities to prioritize goals and initiatives in line with the overarching vision. The vision is inspiring and resonates with the values, aspirations, and needs of community members. Their vision serves as a rallying point, bringing individuals together and igniting a sense of purpose and collective action.

I have seen community leaders use the power of storytelling to effectively highlight the benefits and positive outcomes that can be achieved through collective action. I believe that transformational community leaders know how to encourage individuals to connect their aspirations and values with the community's greater vision, creating a sense of purpose and motivation. This is in part because they can tap into their wells of empathy. They know how to listen to people's needs without judging the people. They can also discern the unspoken needs of the people that they lead by looking at the situations that the people are in and working with the people to develop holistic solutions to the community's challenges. In this way, they validate the viewpoints of the people that they represent.

This is only possible if they also embrace democracy. Unless these leaders encourage all members of the community to speak out freely, express their concerns, and contribute to solving the challenges, the community will still be divided. Being a democratic leader entails reaching out to the marginalized, creating opportunities for them to be heard, and designing systems that ensure inclusivity and equality of all the community's membership. It means mobilizing grassroots support and training community-level organizers to ensure that they involve all parties in decision-making processes, empower them to contribute to the realization of the vision, and provide opportunities for active participation. This fosters a collective sense of responsibility and encourages community members to take ownership of the community's success.

Let me share two stories of my family and our experience with hate and violence in the United States. One story depicts an absence of community leadership, and the other demonstrates the positive impact of community leadership. Democracy does not guarantee peace, but it provides leaders with the opportunity and the freedom to stand together in moments of crisis.

The first story takes place in the early 1990s. My family had just immigrated to the U.S. and settled in a predominantly white community in Denver, Colorado. Ours was the only Muslim, Black, and African family in our neighborhood. The nonprofit Church World Service sponsored my family and was a big help in welcoming us, but my family stood out in town due to our skin color and the Muslim religious clothes worn by my sisters.

My family celebrated when we earned enough money to purchase a car. Once we had it, it was common in the mornings for it to have a flat tire. It was an old, worn, pre-owned vehicle. My siblings would inflate the tire and then get on the road to work.

The flat tire problem persisted but shifted to different tires. Over about a week, my siblings had mended all the tires, but the flat tires continued. It slowly dawned on us that someone was playing a trick on us.

The problem took a new twist. I woke up one morning to find a knife dropped next to the rear flat tire. There was a note too, strategically held into place by the windshield wipers. The note read, "Go back to your country . . . !" It ended by calling us the n-word. This was very frightening, especially to my mother, who was alone at home most of the day.

The note was reported to the police, but there were no suspects. Although the police said they would investigate, my family never saw the police near our home. There was no community response, but the frequency of flat tires decreased.

Then, one Thursday evening as I was having dinner with my family, there was a loud bang as the glass from the living room window shattered and a rock hit the table on which food was being served. This was the scariest experience for us so far since moving to the U.S., but thank God, no one was hurt. My brother immediately called the police, and they responded very quickly. Again, there were no suspects or witnesses, and also no support was provided to our family.

Eventually, my sister Hani identified a teenager from the next-door neighbor's house walking toward our car with a screwdriver. My brother reported this to the police, but my family didn't follow up on the matter. My mother made up her mind to move from the neighborhood for good.

The second story occurred over twenty years later. On August 5, 2017, the darkness of anti-Muslim political violence shook my Minnesota when the Dar Al-Farooq Center was bombed by people trying scare Muslims into leaving the United States. This was a local mosque where my wife, children, and I prayed. No one was physically injured in the attack, but the bombing succeeded in spreading fear.

Three members of a militia group from a small town in Illinois had come to suburban Minnesota outfitted with paramilitary equipment and assault rifles. Their manifesto contained anti-Muslim rhetoric and a call to return to "the good old days." Early on August 5, as the worshippers arrived for morning prayers, these three men had also arrived. Using a sledgehammer, they broke a window into the imam's office at the Dar Al-Farooq Center. They threw in a container of fuel and a twenty-pound, black-powder pipe bomb. The bomb exploded, igniting the fuel mixture and causing fire and smoke damage to the imam's office.

Terrorists had attacked our place of worship. I was an adult now, a leader in the community, and I joined others in speaking out. I had learned by then that democracy requires people to speak up against injustice. Law enforcement responded with arrests and convictions. The mosque also saw support from Minnesotans of many faiths who came together in unity to stand against hate.

These two stories illustrate different reactions to hate-filled violence. When my family was newly arrived in the United States, we were not ready to stand up to our neighbors, and we did not experience community support. Years later, I had the confidence and experience to provide leadership, and I was supported by Christian and Jewish friends who stood with the Muslim community.

The goal of the community is to promote peace and prosperity. This section will explore three practices of community leadership: living with humility, giving everyone a voice, and promoting conflict resolution. These practices create communities where people experience a sense of belonging.

Humility

DEATH IN THE REFUGEE CAMPS

Toward the end of our journey in the refugee camps, my family arrived at Utange in southern Kenya, near the city of Mombasa and the Indian Ocean. My hope rose again in this new camp. I thought my family was safe. My siblings and I even befriended local Kenyans.

With the increase of new refugees, however, the camp quickly became overcrowded, and resources in the region became scarce. My parents scrambled for food and water. Around us, I saw children die of preventable diseases caused by poverty, malnutrition, and poor sanitation. Only a little older than these children and not yet an adult, I felt powerless. So, I prayed.

I always prayed to God. I prayed that one day I would own a business, just as my mom and dad had done. With my money, I would help my parents and other people living on the margins. I knew that fortunes could swing from abundance to abject poverty for reasons beyond people's control; maybe, I thought, the reverse could also happen. My father had had little, and he had built the success of our family.

My dream of saving the lives of my family and neighbors gave me a sense of meaning. Maybe I had a true purpose for living? But then I saw the misery on the faces of family, friends, and strangers, and I wondered if it was impossible for my prayers to be answered. I begged God for a way out, finding a lonely place to hide and cry.

One afternoon, a band of local Kenyans with torches and machetes raided our destitute settlement. They were angry at the Kenyan government for allowing the presence of refugees in the region, but they sought justice by robbing us. They yelled, "Get out of our country, you bloodthirsty savages." The attackers mercilessly slaughtered any refugee who was in their way and set fire to the shelters.

My family was forced to cower in our shelter and pray to Allah. I could not understand the world. I had been ripped away from my toys, my classroom, my ambitions, and my friends. I knew that in other places, children my age were playing video games and soccer in the park. I felt humiliated to be Somali, and anger swelled within me during the attack as I thought about revenge.

Then one person from the hostile tribe, a boy named Salim, appeared at our door and would not leave. He was one of the young locals my brother had befriended. My family did not trust him and feared he would invite our deaths. But Salim insisted that he would protect us. His promise was genuine. He said my family were good people. Though years of harsh living had conditioned us to be distrustful, Salim stood resolute outside our shelter.

My family waited in terror for forty-five minutes while Salim stayed true to his word. The attackers eventually left, sparing our family. When the Red Cross finally arrived, my family stumbled out of our shelter and into a wasteland.

Salim's act of courage—reaching out to protect us despite the hostility from his own people—showed me the power of leading with compassion and empathy even in the darkest of times. It was a lesson I would never forget, and it gave me hope that someday, I too could be a community leader who leads with vulnerability and courage, just like Salim.

Salim risked retribution from his own family for disloyalty. He humbled himself to save us even when we questioned his integrity. It was as if he was driven by something beyond his immediate circumstances. I don't know if he thought about why he did it, but to this day, I believe that Salim embodied something that day that I wish all community leaders could embody: a willingness to weigh all possibilities and do the right thing with courage, even when they are aware of how vulnerable they are.

MARGARET A. CARGILL: EXAMPLE OF HUMILITY

I have always believed in the power of personal stories to change hearts and minds within communities. I have seen how being vulnerable and sharing the difficult experiences of life humanizes people. I had a special opportunity to see that when I worked at Margaret A. Cargill Philanthropies. Let me tell you the story of the organization's founder.

Margaret Anne Cargill was born on January 30, 1920, in La Crosse, Wisconsin. She came from a wealthy family with deep roots in the business world. Her grandfather, William W. Cargill, cofounded the Cargill Corporation, a multinational conglomerate involved in various industries, including agriculture, food production, and commodities trading. Margaret became one of the wealthiest women in the world. How did such a person become an example of humility?

Despite her family's affluence, Margaret led a relatively private and low-profile life. She attended the University of Minnesota and graduated with a degree in English literature. Her passion for philanthropy and helping others began early on, instilled by her parents' belief in giving back to the community. Upon the passing of her father, Paul H. Cargill, in 1960, Margaret inherited a substantial fortune, including a significant stake in the Cargill Corporation. In the years that followed, she became increasingly involved in philanthropy and charitable activities.

With a sincere desire to make a difference and help those in need, Margaret A. Cargill set up Margaret A. Cargill Foundation in 2006. This philanthropic organization was established to carry on her legacy of giving back to society. The foundation's mission is to improve the quality of life for individuals, families, and communities by supporting a wide range of charitable initiatives.

One of the key areas the foundation focuses on is environmental conservation and sustainability. Margaret was a passionate advocate for protecting the environment and ensuring a better world for future generations. The foundation's efforts include supporting conservation projects, promoting sustainable practices, and addressing environmental challenges. In addition to the environment, Margaret A. Cargill Philanthropies supports various other causes, such as education, arts and culture, health, disaster relief, and animal welfare. Margaret believed in the power of philanthropy to create positive change, and she touched the lives of countless individuals and communities through her generosity.

Margaret A. Cargill passed away on August 1, 2006, at the age of eighty-six. Her death marked the end of an era for the Cargill family, but her philanthropic legacy continues to thrive through the work of Margaret A. Cargill Philanthropies.

Today, Margaret A. Cargill Philanthropies remains a prominent philanthropic institution that is dedicated to carrying out Margaret's vision, and to creating positive change in the world, guided by the values of integrity, compassion, and empathy that she exemplified throughout her life. Margaret's philanthropic assets are estimated to be over $9 billion. I was one of the first forty people hired in 2012 to help manage the funds.

In my new position as a senior program officer, I felt a sense of responsibility to uphold the values that guided her philanthropic endeavors.

From the moment I set foot in Margaret A. Cargill Philanthropies, I was struck by the atmosphere of humility that permeated the organization. Despite the immense wealth and resources at our disposal, Margaret's story of humility served as a guiding light for all of us, reminding us that our purpose was not to flaunt the enormous resources we were stewarding but to utilize them wisely and selflessly to help those in need.

Her story also connected with my own cultural background, which emphasized the importance of humility as a virtue. As I was growing up, my family had instilled in me the belief that true success lies not in personal gain but in the ability to uplift others. Seeing Margaret's philanthropic work as an embodiment of this principle filled me with a sense of purpose and pride in the organization I served.

Working at the foundation, I had the opportunity to witness firsthand the impact of our initiatives on communities around the world. Within the United States, I led the foundation's grants to children and families. The projects funded during that time included FOODRx (Second Harvest Heartland's food-as-medicine program), the nutrition program by Youthprise, and the youth employment program at Cookie Cart, as well as the affordable housing programs Aeon and Common-Bond Communities. I also helped direct funding to Twin Cities Public Television, the Wolf Ridge Environmental Learning Center, the Women's Foundation of Minnesota, the American Swedish Institute, and the Courage Center, among dozens of other worthy causes and organizations.

Internationally, I oversaw grants for the provision of nutritious food through household gardens in Bangladesh and, in five Eurasian countries, funds for community childcare centers for children with disabilities. I managed the grant proposal processes and grantee relationships in Laos, Ethiopia, India, Sri Lanka, the Democratic Republic of the Congo,

Indonesia, and the Sicangu Nation (Rosebud Sioux Tribe). I interacted diplomatically and sensitively with the public, community leaders, social service and community-based organizations, national and international agencies like UNICEF, and the American Refugee Committee.

I cannot count how many times I, in my role as a senior program officer, drew on Margaret's story of humility while making impactful decisions. When faced with challenging choices, I sometimes asked myself, "How will this money make a difference?" If nothing else, this approach to philanthropy reminded me to stay grounded, to listen to the needs of the communities we aimed to serve, and to collaborate with humility and empathy.

This took me back to my roots. By the time I was a young man, I had learned that there is more to life and business than survival. I learned this from my parents. Before his death, my father was able to find meaning in life with my mother. He was also able to create more business success within the context of their supportive marriage partnership than he could have on his own. Together they built a large family: sixteen children that included me and my half brothers and half sisters. They also helped support a large extended family.

Beyond supporting the family, my parents' business success also allowed them, as employers and as philanthropists, to make a difference for many. They gave to people in need, welcoming strangers into our home. They supported mosques: the mosque being a place that helped my father as a young man when he was in greatest need. Because of them, I know that from the largest corporate philanthropy to the local charity work of main street stores, the impact of humility in a community leader is seen every day. I watched my parents' success grow, and their humility seemed to grow alongside it.

It was this lesson that guided me later on: when I was appointed by President Biden, for example, but also in many of my other community leadership positions. As the president's appointee, I had to live this rule out. I received overwhelming news coverage in this role, as well as thousands of personal messages and lots of media requests for interviews. All this could have easily gone to my head, but I had long ago learned that all leaders must be humble and vulnerable, particularly now, when social media and technology are adding significant challenges to fame. I have always desired to draw attention to the work I do and not to myself.

I have come to see that humility is not a sign of weakness but a source of strength. It allows us to learn from others, to adapt and evolve our strategies, and ultimately to create more meaningful and sustainable change. Though Margaret had passed away before I joined the foundation, her spirit was alive in every project we undertook. Her story of humility became intertwined with my own, shaping the way I approached my work and life outside the organization. It reminded me that, no matter how successful or accomplished we may become, humility is a constant reminder of our humanity and of our shared responsibility to uplift those in need.

THE SOUND OF MY VOICE

In recent years, the world has witnessed significant events that underscore the urgent need for a fresh approach to leadership. From the crisis in the Catholic Church to ethical lapses in the business community, the war with Ukraine, and ongoing violence in various regions, top leaders' responses have often been characterized by arrogance and defensiveness, exacerbating rather than resolving the situations at hand. Unfortunately, this pattern of betrayal, retaliation, and mistrust has also infiltrated our interactions with authority figures in our work and community lives. If we are to break free from this cycle and adapt to our interdependent world, it is essential that we utilize new leadership approaches.

In this rapidly changing world, leadership should be seen not as a fixed set of qualities but rather as an activity: the art of engaging people to achieve common goals. The effectiveness of leadership styles is influenced by the social, political, economic, and technological environment. It is evident that the environment has shifted dramatically, necessitating the development of new characteristics for effective leadership. One such trait is humility.

A seemingly unconventional leadership trait, humility is not typically associated with the work of managing others. The word itself conjures images of weakness, fallibility, and defenselessness. It might remind you of danger, dependence, exposure, and peril, among other possible threats. Vulnerability is a word that I use to understand humility in action. So, why would anyone willingly choose humility, and how can it be crucial for leaders today?

The practical truth of life is that we're all vulnerable. But many of us spend a lot of effort trying to hide our imperfections instead of just living life to the fullest, despite our vulnerabilities. We get caught up in this relentless pursuit of perfection in our relationships, at work, and even at home. And you know what? It usually just ends up causing stress, anxiety, and even depression. We start judging ourselves and others too hastily. A community leader cannot afford to go down this line.

Brené Brown, PhD, nails it in her book *Daring Greatly: How the Courage to Be Vulnerable Transforms the Way We Live, Love, Parent, and Lead*. She says vulnerability is where all the good stuff happens. It's the birthplace of love, belonging, joy, courage, empathy, accountability, and authenticity. If we want to find our purpose or have more meaningful lives, humility through vulnerability is the way to go. Embracing your true self isn't as hard as it sounds. It's about understanding and accepting yourself. You have to be compassionate with yourself and build on who you are, not try to be something you're not.

Practicing humility is about letting go of selfish pride and arrogant ego. Most often, humility is not about one thing; rather, it confronts a person's desire to be great at everything. A leader with humility can still take action to improve, as well as seek feedback and advice to build on strengths, but their worth as a leader is not defined by their success at a skill. Everyone is worthy of dignity and love, and being a person is enough.

Vulnerability is the real deal. It means being open to both the rough and the beautiful parts of life. Be open, even if it means trembling in your boots a bit. That's when the good stuff comes your way. I used to stress out about my accent when speaking English as a second language. I mean, lots of folks do. But over time, I learned to appreciate it. It's become a part of who I am, and I take pride in it. It doesn't define my worth, and it doesn't stop me from communicating and connecting with others.

When I first started to realize that I spoke English differently, I tried very hard to break free from the phonetic patterns of my native tongue. But no matter how hard I tried, some deeply ingrained speech patterns always gave away that I was a non-native speaker. I felt frustrated at times, thinking that my accent was something I needed to get rid of to communicate better. I came across countless resources that promised to help me sound like a native speaker. While I understood the importance of clear pronunciation for effective communication, I also realized that having an accent was not a weakness but a unique badge of my language learning journey.

My accent represents the hard work I put into learning this new language. The sound of a foreign accent should be respected, as it is evidence of the dedication and effort it takes to master a new linguistic realm as an adult. My accent reflects my cultural heritage and personal history. It is a part of who I am, and in time I started to see it as an integral aspect of my identity, one that adds depth to my connections with various cultures. I know the challenges I had to overcome to learn English, so embracing my accent became a reminder of my intellectual journey and the mental acrobatics I went through to be able to communicate in another language effectively.

Plenty of times, my accent has also been a conversation starter. People get curious about the story behind it. It has opened doors to connect with others on a more profound level so that we can share our cultural experiences. Today I can appreciate that languages are living entities, constantly evolving and adapting. There's no one correct way to speak a language, and embracing my accent means embracing my own interpretation of English. My accent allows me to communicate authentically and share my unique voice with the world. It is an example of me embracing my vulnerability. I appreciate it as a testament to my growth, heritage, intelligence, and individuality. This is the kind of thing living with humility does for a person and their leadership.

Community leaders often find themselves in positions that demand strength, resilience, and unwavering confidence. These demands can make it seem like humility is a weakness. However, it is not. It is a catalyst for empathy, trust, and authentic connection with the community.

The primary goal of community leaders is to foster trust and authenticity among the members we serve. Embracing humility allows us to acknowledge our imperfections, fears, and uncertainties, making us more relatable to the community. When leaders allow community members to see them being open about their struggles, this humanizes them and breaks down the barriers that often exist between leaders and followers. This newfound authenticity lays the foundation for genuine connections and trust, creating a safe space for community members to share their own vulnerabilities and concerns.

When we as community leaders embrace humility, we demonstrate our willingness to understand the challenges faced by our people. In sharing personal stories of triumphs and setbacks, we can relate to the experiences of community members on a deeper level. This humility allows us to make decisions that are more attuned to the needs of the community, leading to policies and initiatives that truly make a positive impact.

It is also true that when community leaders embrace humility, they encourage a culture of support and inclusivity within the community. In an environment where individuals do not feel pressured to hide their weaknesses, vulnerabilities are seen as an opportunity for growth and collaboration. As leaders share their vulnerabilities, they encourage others to do the same, fostering an atmosphere of mutual understanding and support. This sense of belonging can be transformative for individuals who might have felt marginalized or isolated, bringing them into the fold and empowering them to contribute fully to the community.

One of the most courageous acts of humility you can commit is authentically and humbly sharing your personal story. I come from an ancient, rich storytelling tradition. Somalia is often called "the land of poets." One of my favorite poets is Abdullahi Moalin Ahmed, also known as "Dhoodaan." Like my ancestors, he grew up in a family of nomadic shepherds. His poetry uses symbolism and humor to speak critically against the authoritarians. In the face of repression, his words dared to challenge the status quo.

In places like the United States, where there is robust freedom to speak, freedom still requires that people share their stories. There are antidemocratic forces at work that manipulate social media, the news, and storytelling in an effort to make sure the voices of the vulnerable are not heard.

I rarely saw a story like mine reflected in the American media. And so, even though I am not a poet, I wrote my story. In 2014, I published *America, Here I Come: A Somali Refugee's Quest for Hope.* The book is an in-depth telling of my family's journey, from Somalia through the refugee camps to life in the United States. I wrote to inspire the hearts and minds of immigrant youth in their quest for education, as well as to help Minnesotans from the dominant culture understand their new

African neighbors. Telling my story honestly means practicing humility. This includes telling stories of my struggles, my mistakes, and my failures.

In the American media, Somalis are often represented as all being violent and untrustworthy, and as participants in a grand anti-Western conspiracy. This narrative is a lie. Somali Americans are peaceful, reliable, and living the American dream. This lie particularly injures the youngest generation, who are most influenced by American media.

As words of hate were on the rise, I wanted to shield my children, but their lives are full of American YouTube, television, and games. I alone cannot protect the youth from hatred. Instead, I encourage young people to be the authors of the Somali American story. We must invite young people to the table and allow their political voices to counter the messages of hate. There can be no significant progress without young people.

To elevate the youth voice and young people's leadership opportunities—in partnership with my friend, film director James Christenson— I launched *Rumee*, a web anthology series of short films directed, produced, and written by Minnesota-based Somali youth storytellers. *Rumee* pairs these new voices with motivated professional collaborators and mentors. *Rumee*, named for the Somali word that means "to come to believe," addresses the belief gap experienced by Somali youth, by expanding what they imagine they are capable of doing. These young storytellers shared their experiences with humility and purpose. Their stories were a direct challenge to the dominant media narratives about criminal behavior within the Somali community, and about Somali youth being the perpetrators and victims of political violence.

The experience of producing the initial episodes of *Rumee* gave me the confidence to agree to be the subject of one documentary film. Instead of focusing on Somali young adults, this documentary centers on my life and my relationships with my four children: Samia, Subuir, Sabrina, and Suhur. President Donald Trump once declared that Muslim refugee families like mine could be a "Trojan Horse" threat to America.

The documentary humbly demonstrates, by showing my children's different activities, how rooted my family is in the U.S.: from school classes to shoveling Minnesota snow to playing at the Mall of America. The documentary also shows me as a father—*aabo* in Somali—whose love for my American children moved me toward public service.

SHAPE COURAGE THROUGH EMBRACING YOUR VULNERABILITY

Humility is an action of courage where a leader authentically reflects on, and humbly shares, their story. Humility explores both suffering and hope. Leaders with humility enter unafraid into the conversation about struggle, pain, and loss, and they practice simple acts of love and goodness in these difficult spaces.

Humility is the basis on which democracy functions and from which peace is built. With humility, there is a human connection from which to share, to come together as equals, and to compromise as needed. And the stories shared through humility have power. Humility inspires candor and vulnerability, and it demands that those speaking use better words. The words leaders use may be shared softly or loudly, but either way, if they are spoken in vulnerability, change can begin.

In my life, I have experienced the cruelty of leadership that does not include humility. In the refugee camps, I saw children die from preventable diseases because their arrogant leaders had chosen war. Lacking humility, authoritarian leaders are incapable of participatory government and public policy implementation. However, I also saw beauty in the lives of refugees in the camps: people who, while possessing the least, could warmly pass time together, sharing both their trauma and their dreams for a better future. Humility is accessible to anyone.

I am moved by countless leaders who share their stories with humility, including transformational leaders whose stories outlive them, passed on by the people whose lives they touched, and whom they inspired. I try to follow their model of authenticity whenever I report on my work, give a speech, or write an essay about myself. I know that my words are not perfect, and my ideas might be incomplete. Still, I believe that the future, including a robust and lasting democracy, relies on leaders leading with humility.

Do not be afraid of humility. With humility, you learn that life is a gift and that you need to be present to the blessings in your life. Humility helps you to forgive yourself and forgive others. It frees you to acknowledge and let go of your selfishness and your insecurities. When you are a leader with humility, you can let yourself be moved by others. You can choose to be a follower for a time, and then maybe a leader again later. You can pursue the happiness of a higher good that is beyond your individual desires. Humility has so much to offer your leadership.

Here are a few ways to cultivate and leverage humility as a leader:

1. You always have a choice.

Although the tone is often harsh and bleak, I find beauty in Victor Frankl's 1946 nonfiction masterpiece, *Man's Search for Meaning*. In it, he recounts his experiences as a prisoner and forced laborer in a Nazi concentration camp. His book tells of how the most powerless people can survive and how their survival is connected to their ability to find purpose and dignity in the worst of circumstances.

He writes of a memorable experience of human nature in the camps. "We who lived in concentration camps can remember the men who walked through the huts comforting others, giving away their last piece of bread. They may have been few in number, but they offer sufficient proof that everything can be taken from a man but one thing: the last of the human freedoms—to choose one's attitude in any given set of circumstances, to choose one's own way. And there were always choices to make."

His words remind me of some choices that I have faced. Back in

Somalia, my family's stability crumbled abruptly with the civil war in 1991. At some point after the war began, a mortar blew up the nearby electricity transformer and the lights went out in our home. My family was literally without power. The food stored in our freezer started going bad. Without energy to pump water into homes, the stench coming from the washrooms became unbearable.

I understood hunger too. With the food supplies going bad and nowhere to buy replenishments, I survived by skipping meals. I discovered what life was like for the millions of Somali citizens who lived without electricity or running water and with little food. I felt powerless, but even as a boy, I had the choice of how I would respond to this feeling.

Many times a day, you are confronted with choices that invite you to live fully or to resign yourself quietly. You can choose to act powerfully or you can choose to retreat. As Victor Frankl said, there are always choices to make.

2.   Commit to regular reflection.

Make a habit of reflecting on your inner world, especially in times when you have to deal with a potentially divisive issue. We are not in control of the world. We do not always have the right answer.

The word *humility* comes from the Latin word *humus*, which means earth. According to many religious traditions, people were created from the earth, and when we die we return to the earth. Humility is about staying grounded in the earth; it's about not becoming full of ourselves.

There are countless pathways to reflect. Start by reflecting on your own feelings, insecurities, and fears. Recognize that everyone has vulnerabilities, including leaders. For some, reflection is achieved through journaling, conversation, or meditation. For others, reflection comes through rituals and prayer. The name of my faith, Islam, translates to "submission to the will of God." I am called to submit to a higher good that is greater than my desires. Reflection can help those who are used to being in charge see their need for others, for nature, and for a higher power.

Understanding and accepting your own emotions will make it easier for you to relate to others and to create an environment where vulnerability is accepted. One powerful personal discipline I discovered is the practice of breathing in someone's pain and negativity and breathing out warmth and positive energy toward them. This practice helps with cultivating compassion and connection with others, challenging the natural tendency to reject different perspectives. But you can also train yourself to take on different perspectives and roles to see issues from various vantage points. Such exercises are useful not only for teams tackling real problems but also for individuals pursuing personal growth.

3. Share your story.

Share your personal experiences, successes, and failures with your team and the community. By opening up about your journey and the challenges you've faced, you create a safe space for others to share their stories too. But while you're at it, listen actively. Pay attention to the concerns, ideas, and feedback of community members. Show empathy and understanding, even if their perspectives differ from your own. Demonstrate that you value their input and that their voices matter.

Professor Marshall Ganz, a lecturer in public policy at the Kennedy School of Government at Harvard University, writes the following in his article "What is Public Narrative?":

Practicing leadership—enabling others to achieve purpose in the face of uncertainty—requires engaging the heart, the head, and the hands: motivation, strategy, and action. Through narrative, we can articulate the experience of choice in the face of urgent challenge and we can learn how to draw on our values to manage the anxiety of agency, as well as its exhilaration. It is the discursive process through which indi-

viduals, communities, and nations make choices, construct identity, and inspire action. Because we use narrative to engage the "head" and the "heart," it both instructs and inspires—teaching us not only how we ought to act, but motivating us to act—and thus engaging the "hands" as well. . . .

Public narrative is composed of three elements: a story of self, a story of us, and a story of now. A story of self communicates who I am—my values, my experience, why I do what I do. A story of us communicates who we are—our shared values, our shared experience, and why we do what we do. And a story of now transforms the present into a moment of challenge, hope, and choice.

This way of thinking resonates with me greatly because it paints an image of how we all can reimagine the future together: by sharing our individual stories and connecting them in a way that helps us understand why every moment matters.

Conclusion: Leadership with Humility

Universally, leadership with humility lives out the truth that every person is worthy through a leader who accepts their own worth. Acting from their self-awareness and understanding, a leader bravely shares the stories of their journey: their successes and their struggles. When leaders exhibit such behavior, meaningful connections occur. Mutual sharing humanizes each person and can break down the barriers between them. This outcome creates a safe space in which genuine connections and trust are made, allowing for community to form.

Democracy

GETTING OUT THE VOTE

In 1960, Somalis chose to become the first democracy in the continent of Africa. In the 1967 presidential election, the incumbent president, Aden Adde, was defeated by his former prime minister, Abdirashid Sharmarke, and they became the first heads of state in Africa to peacefully hand over power democratically. Two years later, the new president was assassinated, and a military coup d'état led to decades of authoritarian rule. Even though democracy did not last long, these founders left behind a strong democratic legacy as a model of good governance and as a gift to future generations. Since that time, the country's political landscape had been tumultuous, with years of instability and conflict robbing people of the opportunity to experience democratic governance.

In my youth, Somalia was a dictatorship, and the concept of democracy was foreign to me. However, this changed when I moved to California. There, I earned my U.S. citizenship, a milestone that filled me with immense pride and a newfound sense of belonging. With citizenship came the right to vote, and I eagerly awaited the chance to participate in the democratic process. For the first time, my voice would be heard, and my vote would matter. It was a revelation that brought a sense of self-worth and empowerment.

As I headed to the polling station for the very first time, I carried not only my hopes and aspirations but also those of my family and neighbors. In the Somali community, we often felt isolated, but I saw myself as a connector and was determined to bridge the gap between us and the wider society. After the terrorist attacks of 9/11, my passion for encouraging community engagement and participation in democracy had intensified. Activism became a regular part of my life, and I used the Muslim Eid holidays as an opportunity to talk to my fellow community members about the importance of voting, participating in the census, and accessing public resources.

I was particularly driven to empower the youth within the community. I recruited many of my nieces to become election workers, believing that they held the potential to be catalysts for change. Together, we worked tirelessly to increase voter participation, not just within the Somali community but also in the broader San Diego area. Our efforts were fruitful, as we witnessed a rise in voter registrations and a surge in voter turnout during elections. The feeling of seeing our community members actively engage in the democratic process was truly heartening. It was a testament to the power of democracy in shaping our collective future.

Through our activism and commitment to democratic principles, we transformed perceptions of the Somali community so that people saw it not as one of isolation but as one of active participation and contribution. We were no longer on the sidelines; we had a voice, and we made it heard. My journey with democracy had come full circle. I had begun in a place where it seemed like an unattainable dream, Somalia, and now lived in a reality where I, as a college student in California, actively participated in shaping the future of my community through voting and activism. The power of democracy had not only enriched my life but also brought hope and a sense of unity to my fellow community members.

Democratic elections are how the people hire and fire elected officials and decide how public resources are used. This power is why some anti-democratic factions want to restrict voting rights. I am proud of Minnesota's tradition of same-day voter registration. On Election Day, a citizen can both register to vote and cast a ballot. This is one of the main reasons why Minnesota has some of the highest voter turnout in the country. While this is great, I know that my friends and family still face barriers to voting. These include language barriers, lack of transportation, and little knowledge of their rights and how to navigate the voting system.

But democracy is not just useful when it comes to voting. Democracy empowers individuals and fosters a sense of collective responsibility, participation, and representation. It ensures that every member of the community has a voice and the right to participate in decision-making. It promotes inclusivity by representing the diverse perspectives, needs, and aspirations of community members, regardless of their background or social standing.

One way to understand political participation is through the idea of power. Change happens through individuals making a demand for change, communities organizing with a shared demand for change, and the decision-makers agreeing to this change. In a democracy, leaders, communities, and individuals are guaranteed the freedom to make their demands heard. Making a demand for change can be scary and uncomfortable, and it can take years or decades of organizing for change to occur.

In 1857, while slavery was still legal in much of the United States,

Frederick Douglass—a former slave and leading abolitionist—spoke about the essential nature of making a demand, stating: "Power concedes nothing without a demand. It never did and it never will." Douglass spent decades speaking out against slavery. He helped organize abolition societies that were focused on the election of candidates, and he advanced legislation to end slavery. He also lobbied elected officials, including President Abraham Lincoln. Later, after slavery had been made illegal in the United States, Douglass became the first African American diplomat in the U.S., as ambassador to the nation of Haiti.

Douglass set an example as a heroic leader who was making a historic demand, but people make demands all the time, not just leaders. Let me provide you with one example. At the age of five, I identified blue as my favorite color, and I insisted my parents paint the walls of the room that I shared with my brothers blue. Although this might not have been an ideal color to match our home, which was tan colored on the outside, my parents accommodated my demand. In a small way, I experienced my power by asking for something and receiving it.

All people make demands, but democratic community leaders make demands as a way of being accountable to the people they serve. Their leadership is of the people, by the people, and for the people. And to be accountable, democratic community leaders must also be public about their values and their decisions. Transparency in decision-making builds trust and reduces the risk of corruption or misuse of power.

It is democracy that provides community leaders a peaceful and structured framework for resolving conflicts and addressing disputes within the community. Democracy ensures the kind of open dialogue and negotiation that leads democratic leaders to compromise so that they can satisfy various interests and maintain harmony.

Democratic practices empower people to actively engage in shaping their community's future. By participating in elections, voicing opinions, and advocating for their rights, community members become active stakeholders in their own governance. Democracy encourages a sense of unity among community members as they work together to achieve common goals, and it simultaneously respects the freedom of others to dissent. Shared decision-making and collaboration work together to strengthen social bonds and can create a cohesive community.

DEMOCRATIC EDUCATION: NEW YORK CITY TO WILLMAR, MINNESOTA

In 2019, I hopped in a car with my friend Tom Friedman, the *New York Times* columnist I mentioned in an earlier chapter, to head to Willmar: a rural town of twenty-one thousand. Located in the heart of Minnesota farmland, Willmar had welcomed immigrants from Africa, Latin America, and Southeast Asia to meet the workforce needs of the town's turkey processing plants and other agricultural industries. I know Somali families who settled there, and I was in the car to talk, in my role as the deputy commissioner for Workforce Development at DEED, about Minnesota's global workforce needs. I explained to Tom how this small town was responding to global issues like war, climate change, economic uncertainty, and demographics.

Tom brought his personal history with Willmar. Decades before, he had regularly visited his aunt and uncle, who owned a small company there. Tom's previous impression of Willmar was that it was a predominantly white, Lutheran, and Scandinavian town, but this visit inspired him to write a column about the new immigrants who were finding a sense of belonging in rural places. His column regularly celebrated community leaders who applied the democratic values of inclusion and problem-solving.

Tom and I had both been invited to Willmar by Dana Mortenson of World Savvy. Dana is a great friend of mine. World Savvy empowers young people across the United States by giving them the knowledge, skills, and global perspectives they need to become informed and engaged global citizens. Dana introduced Tom to the students and the school leaders of Willmar who were promoting democratic values in their community.

Dana Mortensen is a visionary leader, and her belief in the transformative power of education to bridge cultural divides and build stronger communities shines through everything she does. Driven by her belief in education's power to drive positive change, Dana cofounded World Savvy with a mission to cultivate the next generation of leaders and equip them to tackle complex global challenges with empathy and open-mindedness.

Under Dana's leadership, World Savvy has flourished into a vibrant hub of learning and community engagement. The organization partners with schools, educators, and community leaders, offering transformative programs that integrate global perspectives into the curriculum. One of the key pillars of World Savvy's approach is democracy in action.

Dana firmly believes that young minds should be nurtured within a democratic learning environment, where their voices are heard and their ideas valued. She encourages open discussions, debates, and student-led initiatives that allow young learners to engage critically with global issues and explore diverse perspectives.

World Savvy's impact on students is profound. As young people embrace the spirit of democracy and see community leadership exemplified, they discover their own agency in making a positive difference in the world. They learn to value empathy and to see beyond borders, embracing their roles as global citizens. World Savvy's programs have been expanding, and so have its reach and influence. The organization's impact extends beyond what was expected, touching the lives of students in different corners of the world. Dana's vision of creating a global community of informed and empowered youth is coming to life, and I am grateful to be a volunteer, a collaborator, and a donor to World Savvy.

When I think of the work we have done with the organization, I get more convinced that democratic community leadership is the way to go. One cannot possibly overstate the importance of democracy's role in fostering inclusive and equitable educational systems where every student's potential can be realized, regardless of their background or circumstances.

In many ways, education is a tool for empowerment. Just consider the vital role of community engagement in creating a holistic learning environment, or the importance of involving parents, businesses, and community organizations in shaping educational policies and supporting students' growth beyond the classroom. Whichever angle you approach it from, there is an inevitable connection between education, democracy, and community leadership.

HELPING A FRIEND
BECOME A STATE REPRESENTATIVE

A surprise announcement in December 2017 brought me more into local politics: state representative Karen J. Clark was not seeking reelection. A former nurse, Karen was a legend in progressive politics due to her history of advocating for environmental justice, healthcare, and housing. She was the longest-serving openly lesbian legislator in any state. I knew her district well, and it was one of the poorest and most racially diverse: home to large Native American, Latino, and Somali populations.

Many people asked me to run for her seat, but I understood that women were significantly underrepresented in the legislature. I looked for a progressive female candidate to support, and I helped found Hodan Hassan. Hodan was a great friend and a leader who I had the pleasure of working together with to organize academic conferences for the Institute for Horn of Africa Studies and Affairs (IHASA). A Somali refugee, Hodan had arrived in Minneapolis in 1999 and become a social worker focused on mental health issues. Like me, she had not lived her life to be a politician.

She responded to the call to lead with a *yes*, even though she did not yet have her own political network to run a campaign. I and many others offered our network. I went to work calling for volunteers and money for the campaign. The main job of a candidate is to reach out to people: asking for their vote and asking for their money. Hodan's calendar became filled with conversations, and through these, she built a diverse team of volunteers and supporters. With five strong candidates in the race—three of whom were Somali—Hodan needed to build a network of both East African support and non–East African support. She had a great campaign manager and she earned the endorsement of Women Winning, an advocacy group that promotes and supports pro-choice female candidates.

Hodan inspired voters. She was a great advocate and an immigrant leader who had overcome many barriers. She'd earned a bachelor's degree in social work at Metropolitan State University, and she'd earned her master's in the same subject at Augsburg University. She had lived and worked in the neighborhood for over twenty years. She was a community activist whose life looked like the lives of the people she wanted to represent.

The evening of Tuesday, August 14, 2018, was the most exciting night to date in my emerging life as a political leader. That was the primary election night for the Democratic–Farmer–Labor Party: the left-leaning party in Minnesota. Through my many hours volunteering for Hodan Hassan, I had gained great leadership insights, including the need for leadership voices like mine. I had built a network, and by Election Day, my energy, excitement, and direct asks were resulting in a strong turnout of my friends, family, and strangers to vote for these candidates.

At 8:00 p.m., the polls closed and I was full of nerves. I joined the gathering in the cafeteria of Mercy Mosque, an Islamic center rented as a staging location for volunteers by Hodan's campaign, where an election night results-watching party was being held. With only 28 percent of the vote, Hodan won a closely divided primary, in which four good candidates each got at least 20 percent of the vote. My spirit soared with the cries of joy in the cafeteria. In this district, winning the primary ensured that Hodan would be the next state representative.

On this same night, Mohamud Noor, an active member of the Coalition of Somali American Leaders and the director of the Confederation of Somali Community, won a primary election in Minneapolis's Cedar-Riverside neighborhood to become their next state representative. And state representative Ilhan Omar won a three-way primary with 48 percent of the vote, advancing her toward becoming the next U.S. representative from Minnesota's Fifth Congressional District. Ilhan would become the first Somali American and the first refugee of African birth, and one of the first two Muslim women, to serve in Congress.

For practitioners of democratic community leadership, electoral campaigns are the fertile ground in which the seeds of compassion, empathy, and understanding across multiracial, interreligious, and intergenerational communities can flourish. By reaching out to people and assisting them in achieving their dreams and aspirations, campaigns can create a powerful ripple effect that reverberates throughout the community. The beauty of campaigns lies in their inherent interdependence. As we build new relationships and political power, we open doors to receive support, encouragement, and opportunities in return. Win or lose, this collaborative spirit of campaigns enriches people's lives and unlocks our potential for achieving our biggest dreams.

2020 BIDEN PRESIDENTIAL CAMPAIGN

As the world grappled with unprecedented challenges in 2020, together with a team of similar-minded people, I found myself working to strengthen democracy, in what I now consider one of my successful efforts at it. I found myself with a unique opportunity to contribute to this noble cause by serving on Joe Biden's presidential campaign as an economic policy advisor. The stakes were high, and the responsibility was immense. Our mission was clear: to inspire and mobilize the nation toward a brighter and more inclusive future. As an economic policy advisor, I knew that our policies and plans had the potential to shape the lives of millions and set the course for progress and prosperity.

Antony Blinken, a longtime friend and advisor to Joe Biden and future U.S. Secretary of State, was my first connection to the presidential campaign. Through this introduction to Blinken, I was invited to serve as a volunteer member of the campaign's Economic Policy Committee. I advised the campaign on workforce and economic inclusion, and I spoke on behalf of the campaign, including on a panel discussion for World Refugee Day alongside Samantha Power, former U.S. ambassador to the United Nations and, currently, the administrator for USAID.

We worked tirelessly on the campaign to craft policies that would address economic disparities, promote job growth, and build a more resilient and equitable nation. But our efforts went beyond mere policies and numbers. We sought to inspire a sense of unity and collective purpose, reaching out to communities across the country, listening to their concerns, and understanding their aspirations. Strengthening democracy means ensuring that every voice is heard and every citizen is empowered to participate in shaping their own destiny.

Election Day arrived, and the air was charged with anticipation and hope. As the results poured in, it became evident that our efforts had borne fruit. The people had spoken, and they had chosen Joe Biden and Kamala Harris as president and vice president. Yet, the election was close. With a change of less than sixty-five thousand votes in four states (Wisconsin, Arizona, Georgia, and Nebraska), Donald Trump would have been reelected. I celebrated our victory not just for my candidate, but for our democratic systems: a hard-fought win gained in the midst of a difficult election.

There is still so much that needs to be done to strengthen democracy.

It is an ongoing job that requires continuous effort, engagement, and a commitment to the values that define us as a nation. It is a journey that each of us plays a part in as citizens, as leaders, and as advocates for positive change. Joe Biden's words, spoken at an event in Arizona in 2023, speak to the dangers of losing democracy:

We should all remember, democracies don't have to die at the end of a rifle. They can die when people are silent, when they fail to stand up or condemn threats to democracy, when people are willing to give away that which is most precious to them because they feel frustrated, disillusioned, tired, alienated.

As community leaders, we have to stay committed to the cause of democracy. We have to continually engage with our communities, listen to their concerns, and work toward policies and initiatives that will uplift and empower all.

I often hope that 2020 marked a turning point in our collective journey toward a stronger democracy. Even if it was not, it was a reminder that in times of challenge, we have the power to come together, to lead with compassion and vision, and to build a future where democracy thrives and the voices of all are heard.

One of the key reasons democratic community leadership wins the people is that it emphasizes active participation and decision-making. When community members are involved in the process of shaping policies, they feel a sense of empowerment and agency. Their perspectives, concerns, and aspirations are taken into account. They are heard and understood. This not only builds trust but also creates a sense of ownership and responsibility for the community's well-being.

In contrast to authoritative or autocratic leadership, where decisions are made unilaterally by a select few, democratic leadership seeks consensus and input from a broad range of stakeholders. This collaborative approach encourages innovative solutions and a diversity of perspectives. As a result, policies are more likely to reflect the diverse needs and interests of the community, leading to greater support and acceptance from the people.

Essentially, democratic community leadership embraces both the inspiration of political campaigns and the integrity of political systems. Leaders are required to respect the outcomes of free and fair electoral processes even when they conflict with personal interests. By putting the collective rights of all people first, leaders demonstrate their commitment to the greater good. This respect for democratic elections creates opportunities for emerging leaders to step forward and contribute their unique perspectives and talents. There are times when leaders must speak out against the electoral process, and when communities must organize against injustice and unfairness, but their demands should be rooted in respect for the human rights and political freedom of all.

PRACTICE BUILDING POWER WITH COMMUNITY

Democracy is a way of governing that is of the people, by the people, and for the people. Democracy is how people freely organize communities, protecting the rights of individuals and promoting peace for everyone. It has many expressions, and it continues to evolve. Democracy is an iterative process, and the people who participate create the process, the rules, and the outcomes. Keeping a democracy active requires ongoing participation and leadership.

In my life, democracy began first as a story. When I was a boy, I knew democracy to be a part of the history of Somalia, but democracy had since been lost and a dictator ruled. Later, in the United States, I was eager to vote, but democracy is more than just voting. I got active in my community and encouraged others to participate. The freedom of democracy allowed me to rise from poverty to become a leader in non-profits, business, and government. Democracy ensured my access to public education. Democracy provided a pathway for new immigrants like me to build and use political power and elect people to represent our voices. The values, systems, and practice of democracy allow me to pursue my purpose—furthering an equitable economy and inclusive democracy—and become a global leader for these goals.

Wherever you are in the world, you can practice democratic community leadership. If, like me, you reside in a democracy—no matter how imperfect that democracy may be—you are lucky. You have countless opportunities to learn about and participate in democracy. Use democracy to be a student, whether in school or on your own. Education is a tool for your empowerment. Listen to a variety of people, access information, and learn about the needs of your community. Learn as well through your participation in open discussions, debates, and collective action. If you do not reside in the freedom of a democracy, start your learning process within trusted relationships and small communities. This is where democracy begins.

Democracy needs you, and it requires your active participation in public life. You can teach your community about elections to help rally votes. You can advocate for decision-makers to support policies that do good. You can stand with another person when their dignity is attacked. In democracies, we need to respect the dignity of all people, even those with whom we disagree.

Here are some practices that will help you lead democratically:

1. Know your power.

Power is experienced when you, your community, and your organization successfully demand change. Through my experiences, I have learned five points of power that you can utilize to empower and support your pursuit of success. Examine these points of power for yourself and your community. Ask yourself: Where do you have power? Where can you build power?

First, there's position power, which refers to the authority and decision-making capabilities that come with your title or position. As a leader, you can leverage this power to create opportunities, remove obstacles, and advocate for your team members' needs and aspirations.

Second is task power, which involves having control over a specific task or job. By delegating tasks effectively, providing necessary resources and support, and empowering individuals to take ownership of their work, you enable them to develop their skills, gain confidence, and achieve success.

Third, you can use personal power that stems from your interpersonal skills, leadership capabilities, passion, inspiration, and personal vision for the future. Harness this power to inspire and motivate your community. You do this by setting an example, sharing their enthusiasm, and demonstrating a clear vision. The result is that you create an environment where individuals feel valued, engaged, and inspired to reach their full potential.

A fourth type of power is relationship power. Relationship power involves establishing and nurturing positive connections with others, including individuals who hold influential positions. Leaders cultivate relationships with influential colleagues, mentors, and advocates who can support and champion their community. By leveraging these relationships, they provide additional resources, opportunities, and visibility for the communities' growth and development.

Finally, there's knowledge power, which derives from relevant experience, expertise, and credentials. Leaders recognize the value of their knowledge and expertise and actively share it. By offering guidance, mentorship, and continuous learning opportunities, they empower their team members to enhance their skills, expand their knowledge, and achieve their professional goals.

2. Establish an inclusive vision.

Begin by developing a clear and inspiring vision for the community's future. Identify the community that you intend to organize, and build a list of community members. Involve community members in this process to ensure that the vision reflects the collective aspirations and values of the people. Ensure that you actively engage with community members through various channels, such as town hall meetings, focus groups, surveys, or online platforms. Listen to their concerns, ideas, and dreams for the community. Recognize and appreciate the diversity within the community, and consider the perspectives of individuals from different backgrounds, ages, cultures, and experiences. A diverse range of voices enriches the vision and makes it more comprehensive.

Once you are sure you have listened well, look for common themes and goals among the community members' input. Identify shared values and aspirations that can serve as a foundation for the inclusive vision, and craft a clear and inspiring vision statement that encapsulates the shared goals and values of the community. Ensure that this statement is accessible and understandable to all members, regardless of their background or education level.

3. Empower emerging leaders.

Democracies require that new leaders step forward continually. These leaders include new candidates for office, new people to lead campaigns, new staff at public agencies, and new policy advocates and community organizers at non-governmental organizations. Having democratic community leadership necessitates encouraging and mentoring emerging leaders. Offer support and opportunities for these individuals to take on leadership roles and to contribute their skills and ideas. Help emerging leaders identify what is in their self-interest: what moves them, motivates them, and inspires their action. Help them connect their self-interest to the needs of the community. Make decisions that prioritize the well-being and development of the entire community, not just specific individuals or groups. This culture of mentorship and empowerment ensures the continuity of strong and capable leadership that continues to win the hearts of the people.

4. Value public accountability.

Engage the community in the implementation of plans and projects. Encourage people to volunteer and to be actively involved in initiatives that benefit the community. Take responsibility for the outcomes of decisions and actions, and hold all people responsible for their commitments. Share the community's demands for change with people who possess positional power in businesses, nonprofits, and government. Build relationships with these people, ask for their support, and hold them accountable. Acknowledge mistakes that occur, and learn from them. Be receptive to feedback, and make necessary adjustments based on community input. Make sure that you regularly assess the progress and impact of decisions and initiatives. Celebrate successes and reflect on challenges, and use feedback about both to continuously improve your democratic community leadership.

Conclusion: Democratic Community Leadership

In its truest form, democratic community leadership advances the common good through the work of leaders who organize coalitions of communities to be powerfully heard. People raise their voices together, participating in transparent processes that respect the rights of the individual and promote compromise in decision-making. When leaders exhibit such behavior, communities unite. Leaders advocate for the different dreams and aspirations of people while contributing to social cohesion. Communities and organizations are strengthened by an interdependence that honors the freedom of individuals and teams.

Peace

MY RELATIVE YUSUF

I was not raised to be a political figure. My parents were business owners, and in my early years, I was an aspiring soccer star and disinterested student. Later experiences of violence in my life moved me toward peacebuilding, and as a peace activist post-9/11, I earned a degree in political science. I was prepared to challenge the system, not lead it. In San Diego, after people started floating my name as a possible city council candidate, I chose to leave with my family for Minnesota, where I did a different type of work. In the field of philanthropy, I championed policy advocacy and I was a resource to elected officials, but I was not a politician.

Though I had not envisioned a political career for myself, I had grown up knowing a fine model of an aspiring politician, and his life showed me examples of the real dangers of limited free speech, stolen elections, and political violence. Yusuf Hassan Abdi is my biological relative; we share a great-great-grandfather, but Yusuf's father and my father were like brothers to each other. Yusuf is two decades older than me, and I looked up to him like I would an elder sibling. He had been born in Kenya and dreamed of being a journalist. He traveled to England to earn his bachelor's degree at the University of Middlesex and then traveled to the United States to get a master's in international relations from Tufts University in Massachusetts.

Yusuf became a journalist in the 1970s, first with the Nairobi-based Voice of Kenya and then the London-based BBC. He then cofounded and edited *Africa Events*, a monthly magazine. Later, in 1994, Yusuf began a decade-long career in media relations with the United Nations, serving in places as diverse as Islamabad, East Timor, Kabul, and New York.

When he was working as a journalist, Yusuf's job had depended on respect for the freedom of speech. As political unrest and repression increased in Kenya, he was targeted as an agitator. He cofounded the Committee for the Release of Political Prisoners, exposing human rights abuses by the Kenyan government. As a result of this activism, in 1987 the Kenyan government revoked his passport and arrested his father. From his example, I saw the consequences of speaking out.

Hoping to build on his successful career as a journalist and diplomat, the Somali community in Nairobi asked him to run for the Kenyan parliament. In 2007, Yusuf stood for election and won—but political corruption resulted in a rival being seated instead. Yusuf subsequently switched parties, and he came in third in a December 2007 special election that was marred by stolen ballot boxes. Through his example, I saw how corruption can prevent ethical candidates from serving the people.

Undeterred, Yusuf stood for office a third time in August 2011 and secured the win. After he'd served in office a little over a year, on Friday, December 7, 2012, Yusuf met with two hundred supporters who'd gathered after prayers at the Hidaya Mosque in Nairobi. Two children ran up to greet him, and just as they did, someone detonated a bomb constructed of ball bearings and nails. Eight people were killed, including the two children, who had shielded Yusuf from the worst of the bomb. Yusuf was subsequently transported to the hospital, where he nearly lost both legs.

His attackers were never positively identified, but it was clear that anti-peace elements were behind the attempt to assassinate him. He is a moderate Muslim and the first Somali to be elected from Nairobi. In Yusuf's example, I saw the danger of political violence. Although Yusuf was reelected in 2013 to a second term as a member of parliament, his campaign supporters had to carry his banner, as he was recuperating and grieving.

RESOLVING CONFLICT IN EAST AFRICA

In 2008, fueled by a quest for lasting peace and development in the Horn of Africa, I founded the Institute for Horn of Africa Studies and Affairs (IHASA): a think tank dedicated to demystifying conflicts and fostering peace in the Horn of Africa region. IHASA has become a platform for scholars, community members, and international stakeholders to engage in fruitful discussions on socioeconomic and political issues plaguing the region. At IHASA, our approach to leadership has been deeply rooted in democratic principles. We prioritize inclusivity, transparency, and collaboration, ensuring that all community members, regardless of their nationality, have a say in shaping the institute's vision and initiatives. We believe that an inclusive approach leads to comprehensive regional peace, security, and economic integration.

One of IHASA's core goals is to analyze the root causes of conflicts in the Horn of Africa and devise strategies for a sustainable post-conflict era. Through our research and policy work, we provide credible and independent assessments of the political situation and investment opportunities in the region. This has attracted considerable international attention and empowered both Americans and Africans to invest in the region with greater confidence. IHASA's annual academic conference is a hallmark event that has brought together scholars, community members, and leaders to engage in dialogue, exchange knowledge, and foster networks. We also prioritize training young people in conflict analysis and leadership, preparing them for upcoming leadership roles in their communities.

The impact of IHASA's work has been far-reaching. By promoting good governance and democratic systems, the organization fosters a sense of ownership and legitimacy among community members, ensuring that the people's voices are heard and respected. It collaborates with various think tanks and organizations, such as the Wilson Center and the Alliance for Peacebuilding, to promote regional peace in the Horn of Africa. IHASA actively engages in transitional justice initiatives, empowering Somali women to have a greater say in national issues. We recognized that women's voices are often underrepresented in decision-making processes, and we want to bridge this gap and promote gender equality in the region.

Through IHASA's dedication to peacebuilding, we aim to create a region that is resilient, peaceful, and integrated economically. Our mission extends beyond research and policy work, as we conduct free workshops to empower youth with conflict analysis skills and to emphasize the importance of advocating for peace. As IHASA continues to grow, our influence in shaping the thoughts and discourses surrounding the Horn of Africa has expanded. The institute's publications on the state of peace and development in the region have garnered attention from key elected officials and their congressional staff. This led to opportunities for me to participate in congressional briefings, where I advocated for peace and stability in the Horn of Africa.

Above all, IHASA serves as a testament to the power of community organizing and the impact that an inclusive, democratic approach can have in fostering lasting peace and development. Through collaboration, research, and commitment to peace, we strive to make a positive difference in the lives of people in the Horn of Africa and the wider diaspora community.

It was through IHASA that I came to meet a wonderful man who helped broker peace between Ethiopia and Eritrea in the 1990s. His name is Charles "Chic" Dambach, and he is a retired chief of staff for Congressman John Garamendi and former president and CEO of the Alliance for Peacebuilding, which I later joined as a board member. Over the course of his career, Chic has helped to establish extensive networks of organizations and professionals aimed at promoting and creating peace and security worldwide. This great soldier of peace was to become my mentor, and it is he who introduced me to the concept of peacebuilding. (In fact, he is the one who helped popularize the word *peacebuilding*.) He has come to be a great personal friend and a resource for IHASA.

Peacebuilding includes a wide range of efforts by diverse actors in government and civil society at the community, national, and international levels to address the immediate impacts and root causes of conflict before, during, and after violent conflict occurs. Peacebuilding ultimately supports human security: a condition under which people experience freedom from fear, freedom from violence, and freedom from humiliation.

Peacebuilding efforts aim to manage, mitigate, resolve, and transform central aspects of conflict through official diplomacy and civil-society peace processes, as well as through informal dialogues, negotiations, and mediations. Peacebuilding addresses the root causes of violence and fosters reconciliation to prevent the return of instability and violence. Peacebuilding efforts seek to change beliefs, attitudes, and behaviors, and to transform dynamics between individuals and groups, leading them toward a more stable, peaceful coexistence. Peacebuilding also helps to create structures and institutions that provide platforms for the nonviolent resolution of conflict and that stabilize fractured societies.

Since completing advanced training in conflict analysis and resolution from the United States Institute of Peace, I have taken up the challenge to provide free workshops to youth, focusing on conflict analysis training, conflict resolution, and the importance of advocating for peace. I am to this day very passionate about this role, given the devastating effects of war that caused my family to come here as immigrants. Over the years, I have devoted a lot of my energy, resources, and leadership to peacebuilding initiatives through IHASA. Since its formation in 2008, IHASA has become one of the leading think tanks on issues related to the Horn of Africa.

ADVOCATING FOR PEACE IN THE U.S.

The 2021 January 6 attack on the U.S. Capitol, also known as the Capitol riot, was a violent and unprecedented event in Washington, DC, that occurred during the joint session of Congress convened to certify the Electoral College vote count for the 2020 presidential election. The attack occurred at the iconic building that houses the legislative branch of the U.S. government. It was instigated by a mob of supporters of the then-president, Donald Trump, who had refused to accept the results of the 2020 election, falsely claiming widespread voter fraud. Trump had been encouraging his supporters to protest the certification of the election results and had spoken at a rally near the White House on the morning of January 6.

Following the rally, thousands of Trump supporters marched to the Capitol and breached its security barriers, storming the building and clashing with law enforcement officers. The rioters vandalized the Capitol: breaking windows, looting offices, and defacing walls. Inside the Capitol, the joint session of the U.S. Congress was forced to suspend the certification process and evacuate. During the attack, there were moments of violence and chaos. Several people were seriously injured, including law enforcement officers, and multiple rioters and officers lost their lives.

The attack shocked the nation and the world, and it was widely condemned by politicians from both parties and by leaders around the globe. It was a direct assault on American democracy and the peaceful transfer of power, as the certification of Electoral College votes is a ceremonial process that had taken place without interruption in the past.

In the aftermath of the attack, multiple investigations were launched, and authorities arrested and charged many of those involved in the riot. The attack also led to the second impeachment of President Trump by the House of Representatives, on the charge of incitement to insurrection. He was later acquitted by the Senate. The January 6 U.S. Capitol attack underscored the fragility of democracy and the importance of upholding the rule of law and peaceful political processes. It served as a stark reminder of the need for unity, and of the need for respect for the democratic principles that have been the foundation of the United States for centuries.

The United States House Select Committee to Investigate the January 6th Attack on the United States Capitol brought to light a concerning reality: dangerous conflict dynamics are rapidly increasing within the United States. White supremacist and militia groups pose the most significant threat to peace and security, according to U.S. intelligence assessments. While law enforcement plays a crucial role in preventing domestic terrorism and violent extremism, a multifaceted approach that involves civil society and evidence-based programming is required. As conflict dynamics continue to escalate, urgent action is needed to address the root causes and build resilience within the nation.

Regrettably, conflict dynamics in the U.S. are on the rise. The nation's peace and security rankings have been in consistent decline on the Fragile States Index and the Global Peace Index. In 2021 and 2022, the U.S.

experienced political violence, attempts to delegitimize the election process, and worsening social cohesion. These deteriorating indicators underscore the urgency of addressing the underlying factors that are fueling conflict.

In addition, democratic trends in the U.S. have suffered. The Economist Intelligence Unit, the research analysis division of the Economist Group media company, classifies the U.S. as a flawed democracy due to the factors of extreme polarization and gerrymandering. In 2021, the International Institute for Democracy and Electoral Assistance added the U.S. to a list of "backsliding" democracies, citing election disinformation, voter disenchantment, and authoritarian tendencies. This erosion of democratic values further contributes to the escalating conflict dynamics within the nation.

Preventing violent conflict and extremism necessitates a comprehensive and evidence-based approach. Civil society plays a vital role in conflict prevention and peacebuilding, but resources must be strengthened to address the gravity of the current threat. Private donors, corporations, and the U.S. government must increase their support for robust programming designed to prevent and reduce conflict. Additionally, building resilience will require that community leaders have an inclusive vision and commit to addressing the root causes of conflict. It is essential that spaces be created for open dialogue and community engagement, where we can focus on common values that bind the nation together. Education and awareness campaigns that promote understanding and empathy can counter the divisive narratives perpetuated by extremist groups.

A CALL FOR PEACE

There are many places in the world, including the United States, where escalating conflict dynamics have reached a critical point. These times demand urgent attention from policymakers and citizens alike. Conflict and peacebuilding experts have long warned about dangerous trends.

Consider the fact that there is a complex web of factors contributing to rising conflict dynamics. Conflict occurs between countries and communities, but it often begins between individuals. Kofi Annan, former secretary-general of the United Nations, made this point when he received the 2001 Nobel Peace Prize. In his acceptance lecture, he stated, "Peace belongs not only to states or peoples, but to each and every member of those communities. . . . Peace must be sought, above all, because it is the condition for every member of the human family to live a life of dignity and security." When working to prevent conflict, community leaders must not forget the basic needs of individuals.

One way to prevent violent conflict is by learning from experts about the steps of analyzing systemic conflict dynamics and providing early warnings. A conflict assessment entails identifying the indicators that are driving grievances and resiliencies, understanding the actors who are influencing violence or peace, and recognizing potential triggering events that may spark violence. Conflict drivers are multifaceted and involve emotional elements and perceptions that may not be fully rational.

Despite the increasing evidence of rising conflict dynamics all over the world, it can be easy to prioritize immediate crises over prevention and peacebuilding efforts. This shortsighted approach must change, and community leaders must be allocated to address the root causes of conflict. Though meeting individuals' basic needs is crucial, it is equally vital that all significant grievances be addressed, even if they challenge your values and worldview. Grievances can be diverse and competing, and you must hear the lived experiences of all communities.

Community leaders do not need to work alone in building peace; they should partner with formal and informal institutions that play a vital role in suppressing or resolving conflicts through nonviolent means. Countries need strong systems that support compromise, including both formal government institutions and political parties. With public trust in democratic governments near historic lows, peacebuilding efforts benefit when local leaders practice democratic values and work to strengthen social cohesion.

It doesn't help matters that misinformation is being disseminated, especially through social media. The online platforms and a proliferation of weapons together facilitate the spread of radical ideologies, contributing to the radicalization of extremists. Enemies to stability and democracy exist, and sustained peace requires active leadership. The pursuit of peace requires that peacebuilders get on the game field and lead.

PROMOTE BELONGING DURING CONFLICT

Peace is the outcome of individuals' humility lived out through democratic values and practices. Meaningful and lasting peace is not merely a treaty between two nations or two groups that cease fighting. In situations of conflict, lasting peace comes when individuals mutually acknowledge and respect each other's humanity and then come together in their communities to practice peace together. Even in places ruled by authority and oppression, average people can make peace with each other using the values of democracy.

I was formed by the example of many peacebuilders in my own family, including my relative Yusuf Hassan Abdi. In my life, and with this book, I hope to pass on this blessing to my children and to future generations. My personal experiences with violence in Somalia, Kenya, and the United States have deepened my commitment to peace. The Institute for Horn of Africa Studies and Affairs (IHASA) is one way that I help build peace, but I try to practice peace throughout my life.

One way I practice peace is by encouraging the voices of women and youth. They are too often underrepresented in decision-making processes. The world needs a new generation of peacebuilders. No matter what your background or identity, your leadership is needed for peace. You can start in your own life, by embodying peace in your breath, words, and actions. Find a sense of belonging in your life, starting with feeling love and appreciation for yourself. Seek out individuals and communities with whom you can be yourself. Leaders for peace actively encourage communities and individuals to belong to each other and the world. To offer this kind of leadership, you must understand the spaces and relationships where you experience belonging.

Here are a few ways to foster peace in your leadership work:

1. Promote collective wisdom.

All people can live in peace, but the culture and traditions of each community can provide unique pathways to that goal. Consider: How does your community make peace? Breathe. Find peace in yourselves. This might not be easy. In times of conflict, our minds can rage with a deluge of emotions. Help your community to feel its emotions. These may include hostility, anger, frustration, irritation, aggravation, and judgment. People may feel hurt, sadness, concern, disappointment, shame, betrayal and guilt, sympathy and respect, and fear. Facilitate the experience of the conflict. Prepare the community for dialogue. Help members see themselves in the community's wise tradition of peacebuilders.

An example of this type of community preparation for peace is found in the leadership of South African president Nelson Mandela. He led his nation through a transformative moment, advancing the equality of all South Africans and the end of a racial apartheid system. Mandela provided the institutional leadership for a truth and reconciliation process, but he also understood that for national stability to be achieved, all South Africans needed to be peacebuilders. In his inaugural speech as president, Mandela spoke of justice, peace, and the meeting of basic needs for all, but he also challenged individuals to do their part in making peace, stating, "The body, the mind, and the soul have been freed to fulfill themselves." Leaders help people see their ability to make peace.

2. Foster friendships and alliances.

Explore communities that are unknown to you. Attend cultural celebrations and community dialogues and introduce yourself to new people, and bring your friends and family. Going to new places requires that you keep an open mind to different values and ideas. You do not need to sacrifice your values to listen to new people. Respect differences. Build meaningful and trusted relationships. Invite people to your cultural celebrations and community events. Warmly welcome new people who visit your community, and connect them to others in that community.

Grow friendships outside of conflict situations. Be gentle with yourself and with others. Building relationships can be difficult even in times of peace. Forgive yourself and forgive others. Practice acknowledging disagreements and forgiving others in small conflicts. The practice of forgiveness in small things builds your capacity to forgive in more significant conflicts.

Enjoy shared community experiences: food, music, nature, ideas, stories, and goals for the future. Engage in community improvement projects together. Extend your friendship to one another's family, friends, and professional networks. Researchers who have looked into the subject say that a bond between two individuals forms when they can see each other's humanity and, in that vision, recognize their own. In the words of C. S. Lewis, friendship is born the moment when one man, perceiving a shared commonality, says to another, "What? You too?"

3. Be a bridge for divided communities.

Community leaders must be attentive to those who are experiencing, or are at risk of experiencing, domestic violent extremism. Focus on reducing extremist recruitment and facilitating rehabilitation, and apply a public health model that addresses mental health needs in order to prevent violence. Showcase the importance of localized interventions. Leaders can inspire hope, and they can address specific grievances and vulnerabilities that drive violent extremism.

Promoting social cohesion and constructive dialogue is crucial in bridging societal divides and fostering tolerance and cooperation. Create safe spaces for diverse identities to engage in dialogue and deepen understanding. Community leaders can facilitate conversations that bring together individuals from different backgrounds, encouraging mutual respect and empathy, while addressing the root causes of conflict.

4. De-escalate hate.

Educate your community about hate speech. Teach others how to identify misinformation and radicalization. Empower people to speak out against hate in their human interactions. Build up digital literacy among your family and friends. Avoid amplifying digital hate speech. Promote uses of digital spaces that promote belonging. Challenge authority and political leaders without dehumanizing them.

When encountering hate-filled words, and verbal or written aggression, your first action should be to respond to yourself. Breathe. Consider: Are you physically safe? Can you leave this space, the conversation, the online post? What thought or action can help bring you calm? Remember that you are loved. The purpose of hate is often to create more hate. If you can stop yourself from responding with anger immediately, you could prevent accelerating the hate-filled situation.

Other questions you may ask yourself include: Do others need your immediate attention? Do others need help stepping away from the situation? Do they need time to feel loved and supported? In the moment of hate, it is often not possible to reason with or problem-solve with the person who is enraged. But you can be there for others who are affected.

If you do choose to engage with the person who is enraged, and if you are in a place of safety, take time to listen. Ask questions. Be empathetic. If you want a person to change, to grow, and to be better, don't start by attacking them. Peace is built in meaningful relationships. You can be honest about what others have said and what they have done. You should hold leaders accountable and be held accountable yourself.

Peacebuilding requires more than accountability, however. You need to be a leader who listens to others' stories—stories that might be hurtful and wrong—and then shares your truth. It is hard work, and you might not be successful. You don't have to always be the peacebuilder. This is exhausting work, and it is best when the work of making peace is shared among a community of leaders.

The United Nations (UN) suggests an eight-step process for addressing hate speech: pause, fact-check, react, challenge, support, report, educate, and commit. They also support a #PledgeToPause initiative, which encourages people to think before sharing information (or potential misinformation) online. The UN asks individuals to "refrain from making any hateful comments yourself and/or relaying such content." Small amounts of misinformation can have big consequences, and the UN also asks people to use an online search engine to verify the accuracy of hateful information.

Keeping all this in mind, you can then speak up calmly about the hate speech, making it clear that you disagree with the statement. As a next step, you can share positive messages. The UN recommends countering hateful content with positive messages "that spread tolerance, equality, and truth in defense of those being targeted by hate."

You can further find ways to personally support the people who are targets of hate speech. Most online media have policies regarding hate speech, and you can report the posts to administrators or moderators. Finally, you can educate your family and friends about your leadership, and you can commit to joining an organization that addresses hate speech in your community.

Conclusion: Leadership for Peace

When relationships fracture, leadership for peace is empathetic and democratic, offering ways to be a leader who promotes a sense of belonging in response to conflict. Leaders engage in dialogue with all parties to manage, mitigate, resolve, and transform the root causes of grievances. When leaders exhibit such behavior, they choose attitudes and build structures that bridge differences. Peacebuilders are leaders who practice nonviolence, welcome stable coexistence among adversaries, and pursue truth and reconciliation that heals. Human connections can be fragile, and it takes wisdom for individuals, organizations, and people to find agreement.

Conclusion

The morning that I arrived in Washington, DC, to begin my work at the State Department, my Uber driver asked me, "Are you Somali?" I answered that I was.

My driver continued, telling me, "Somali immigrants are becoming more powerful in the United States. Biden even appointed a Somali guy recently!"

This was my informal welcome to my public service work as senior advisor to the U.S. State Department, and as a presidential appointee of President Joe Biden and Vice President Kamala Harris. With this acknowledgment from a stranger, I felt like I was in the right place!

For two years, my leadership as a diplomat and foreign policy professional was tested. In the following paragraphs, I reflect on my time in the federal government. I use my twelve practices for transformational leadership, which I explored in this book, as a framework. My experiences included leading at the levels of community, organization, team, and self. A transformational mindset aided me in translating intangible organizational and societal challenges into tangible solutions and impact.

There are some stories that I cannot share. Working in national security and diplomacy requires a high level of discretion and confidentiality. However, I hope that the following stories will entertain and inspire. As leadership author and expert John Maxwell said in one of his podcasts that I listened to, "I am not going to teach it unless I live it." Using my example, leaders can embrace their potential to create an exponential impact on the prosperity of their organizations and on society. I encourage you to follow this framework and reflect on your leadership using these twelve practices.

LEADING FOR COMMUNITY: PEACE, DEMOCRACY, AND HUMILITY

Seeking Peace in Palestine and Israel

When transformational leadership is applied to communities, **peace** is the result. When this leadership fails, war, violence, and oppression occur. This is what happened in Somalia, where I experienced the impact of violent extremism, and where innocent family members, friends, and relatives of mine were murdered. Peace calls for effective solutions from leaders. Sustainable peace requires a political solution, and I am confident that the efforts of public servants within governments make a difference in most cases.

This confidence is what led me to join the State Department, where I could bring my more than twenty years of experience in peacebuilding to the work of advancing the goal of global peace. In the Biden administration, I joined with other presidential appointees from a range of religious backgrounds—including Muslim, Jewish, Christian, and no religious affiliation at all—in advocating for peace. Yet, as I approached the conclusion of my two years as a presidential appointee, my colleagues and I felt saddened by the devastating violence that reemerged in the Middle East.

On October 7, 2023, Hamas waged a terrorist attack in Israel that resulted in the deaths of over 1,200 people and in the injury and captivity of many civilians. In the immediate aftermath of this tragedy, I reached out to friends and family; to Palestinians and Israelis; to Jews, Christians, and Muslims. I reached out to be present for their pain and listen to their fear. I shared the following quote, attributed to Audrey Hepburn, a refugee from the Nazi invasion of the Netherlands during World War II who became an award-winning actress and a goodwill ambassador for the United Nations International Children's Emergency Fund (UNICEF). These words are essential for building peace: "Nothing is more important than empathy for another human being's suffering. Nothing. Not career, not wealth, not intelligence, certainly not status. We have to feel for one another if we are going to survive with dignity." To get to peace, a person must see the humanity of the other.

The response of the Israeli government to the October 7 attacks—a response supported by the United States—failed to recognize the humanity of innocent Palestinian people. For me, this was a moment of moral crisis. Many federal officials were asking: How can we represent the United States government at this time of failure?

Some officials resigned from the State Department. This included a colleague whose job was to approve the transfer of additional military equipment to Israel. Some people, including members of my family, called on me to resign, but I saw an opportunity to demonstrate leadership in action. Individuals like me are needed to speak out inside the administration. I asked the State Department and White House to adopt new policies that encouraged peace.

Within a democracy, peacebuilding—like all issues—is the work of compromise. The first days and weeks after October 7 were especially painful. As the Israeli government increased attacks in Gaza—particularly the bombings of refugee camps, schools, and hospitals—I had difficult conversations and shared my experience as a peacebuilder.

I found a common cause with Muslim and Jewish appointees. Many of my fellow presidential appointees who are Muslim organized inside the administration to make the case for peace. Our voices were listened to by the White House, including at a much-needed conversation with President Biden's senior staff that included Chief of Staff Jeff Zients, Second Gentleman Doug Emhoff, and other senior officials. Some of the most effective advocates for peace were Jewish Americans who knew that the continued killing of innocents would bring sustainable safety and security to neither Israelis nor Palestinians.

This internal organizing made a difference, and the policy of the United States improved, but efforts to strike a permanent cease-fire did not succeed. On November 14, 2023, I joined hundreds of U.S. officials from forty different agencies in signing a letter to the president, calling for an immediate cease-fire in the Gaza Strip and increased humanitarian aid to Palestinians.

A Global Declaration for Democracy

In my work as a senior advisor for **democracy**, every day of my almost two years included promoting and protecting democracy at home and abroad. The work of democracy is always difficult. In democracy, people come together to speak their truth, to respect others, and to build a way forward through compromise. At this moment in our global affairs, many people are attracted to dictators and to authoritarian leadership. By entering into the president's administration, I joined him in taking a stand for global democratic leadership.

In March 2023, I was part of a historic moment: the endorsement of the Global Declaration of Mayors for Democracy by leaders from seventy-four nations. Despite significant regional, national, cultural, and social differences, leaders from these democratic countries came together to demonstrate support and commitment to the universal value of democracy. As part of an international team, I spent over a year building momentum and goodwill that resulted in the declaration. Democracy is needed to fight authoritarianism, battle corruption, and respect human rights—and the declaration makes that case.

I participated in many conversations and activities around a Year of Action for democracy, and many of those focused on efforts to build the political will in support of the declaration. My colleagues and I invited governments, businesses, labor unions, and nonprofit organizations to demonstrate their support for democracy. We brought people together to have thoughtful discussions. I helped elevate the voices of youth and women, and of communities that are historically excluded from political participation. One product of these efforts was an integrated, comprehensive anti-corruption plan—designed by participants from over forty countries—that promotes transparency, civic participation, and public accountability.

The foreign policy of the United States can be used as a tool to support democracy in other countries. In 2022, ahead of presidential elections in both Somalia and Kenya, I was interested in how the United States would use its influence to encourage democracy. At one point, Secretary of State Antony Blinken took steps to ensure a timely election in Somalia by placing visa restrictions on those individuals known to have undermined Somalia's democracy process. Blinken said, "The United States strongly supports the Somali people and their commitment to democracy." I learned much from working with Secretary Blinken and Under Secretary Uzra Zeya.

That same year, domestically, the people of the United States took a stand for democracy. In November 2022, voters across the country turned out with high levels of voter participation. In many local and state races, voters rejected antidemocratic candidates who embraced the "Big Lie"—the false claim that the 2020 presidential election was stolen from Donald Trump—and who supported authoritarian rule. I was inspired by the voters and by the election system that Americans use to protect their rights and their democracy.

While I celebrate democracy, I acknowledge that the practice of democracy must be reinvented as culture and technology change. In my federal role, I advocated for new approaches and initiatives to advance inclusive democracy, both at home and globally. I also helped elevate global voices to support rising thought leaders for democracy.

As a staff member for the 2023 Summit for Democracy—an in-person and virtual gathering of world leaders—I was pleased that the United States decided to make the summit more inclusive by cohosting with four other nations, including two nations from the global south: Costa Rica, Zambia, the Netherlands, and the Republic of Korea. It is my strong belief that for democracy to endure, the leadership for democracy must be global.

My Voice among Many Stories

When I joined the Biden-Harris administration, I agreed to a code of conduct that limited the expression of my voice. As a representative of the United States, I needed to be prudent with my words. I needed to be careful that my opinions were not confused with the policy of the U.S. federal government. Also, my job responsibilities exposed me to confidential information that I am prevented from sharing. This is not unique to federal service. Many people have jobs and volunteer roles that limit what they can share.

Humility is the practice of creating space for the needs of the community. It allows leaders to let go of some arrogance and self-centeredness. It appreciates the stories and the needs of others. The shared goals of peace and democracy are more important than a desire to publicly say anything in my mind. My needs for self-expression must be shared with the needs of the community.

In this time of limitations on my speech, I grew to appreciate those occasions when I could share my story. Humility includes vulnerably sharing my stories, especially in ways that welcome others to share theirs. Shortly after arriving in the nation's capital, I was invited to be the keynote speaker for the Minnesota State Society in Washington, DC. It was nice to connect to others who were connected to Minnesota.

At other times, I prioritized the opportunity to talk with youth. Spending time with young people is a real joy. At the Aspen Institute's Aspen Leadership Salon, I sat at a roundtable sharing stories with young leaders. Aspen had invited me to talk about my leadership journey and how I navigate change and identity in my work. Honestly, like any good teacher, I learned more from engaging with the students than I did from preparing or teaching my lessons. At the roundtable, I heard someone say, "We need to focus on protecting our democracy; we can't just assume it will be in place in the future unless we work on it right now." I couldn't agree more.

I spoke to national audiences through events organized by Generation Citizen, Alumni Thematic International Exchange Seminars (Alumni TIES), NationSwell, Muslim Americans in Public Service (MAPS), and the Council on Foreign Relations. I told my family story; I spoke about being a refugee from a civil war and about being Black and Muslim in the United States. I shared my ideas about transformational leadership. Many of the ideas and examples shared in this book were tested in conversations with these groups and many others.

LEADING IN ORGANIZATIONS: PROSPERITY, INNOVATION, AND ASSETS

Working for an Equitable Economy from the White House

As a presidential appointee, I worked at a job housed in the State

Department, but I represented the interests of the president. As a result, my work regularly connected me with the staff and the priorities at the White House. While the United States is a global leader on many economic issues, the president's leadership demonstrates his care about the needs of regular people. He grew up without wealth and privilege. When the president thought about **prosperity**, his goal was an equitable economy: one in which people could find good jobs, get an education, and retire well.

Following leadership from the White House, all of President Biden's presidential appointees prioritized an equitable economy in our work. Specifically, my work supported Uzra Zeya, the under secretary of state for the Office of Civilian Security, Democracy, and Human Rights. She traveled the world, building relationships with government, civil-society, business, and union leaders. Raising global labor standards benefited workers in the United States and contributed to economic justice everywhere.

Initially, the economic policies we worked on focused on restoring the jobs lost during the pandemic. This goal was achieved less than two years into the administration. As the economy improved, we celebrated a national unemployment rate of 3.7 percent: the lowest in fifty years. To these efforts, I had brought experience in employment and economic development gained in Minnesota, a state that recorded a 1.8 percent unemployment rate, the lowest in the nation.

These achievements were not enough. People were still struggling to benefit from the economy, and the president challenged his team to do more. He shared these words of inspiration with us upon signing the Inflation Reduction Act of 2022: "This Administration began amid a dark time . . . a 'once-in-a-century pandemic,' devastating joblessness, and threats to democracy and the rule of law, doubts about America's future itself. And yet, we've not wavered. We've not flinched, and we haven't given in. Instead, we're delivering results for the American people."

While my daily job tasks took place on the seventh floor of State

Department headquarters in DC's Foggy Bottom neighborhood, visits to the White House provided important opportunities to build relationships. While I value virtual meetings, relationships can be strengthened through in-person conversations and shared participation in events.

It was an honor to be at the White House for the passage of the previously mentioned Inflation Reduction Act, the hallmark legislation of the president's economic agenda. The act lowered prescription drug costs, invested in new energy technology, and reduced the federal deficit. Partnerships for global trade are essential for prosperity, and I also joined the team to welcome heads of state to the White House, including the president of South Korea and the prime minister of Australia. In addition, after thirty years of federal inaction on the problem of gun violence, I was at the White House with my colleagues to celebrate the passage of the Bipartisan Safer Communities Act in the summer of 2022.

Part of prosperity is enjoying life, and I am grateful to President Biden and First Lady Jill Biden for opening the White House for celebrations. The previous president had eliminated the annual celebration of Eid al-Fitr, the feast that ends the month of Ramadan. Now, President Biden welcomed Muslim elected and appointed officials from across the United States. It was a joy to celebrate with him.

My time in Washington, DC, also saw the first celebration of Juneteenth as a federal holiday. Juneteenth is about equity and commemorates the expansion of freedom and rights to former slaves. Another personal highlight was the tour of the White House that my wife Ikran and I took when she visited me. The history and the hospitality of the White House were an inspiration as I worked to improve people's lives.

Refugees and Immigrants Make a Difference

Angelina Jolie, award-winning actor and a special envoy to the United Nations High Commissioner for Refugees, arrived at our offices in the State Department during my second month in Washington, DC. She came to our Office of Civilian Security, Democracy, and Human Rights to speak on behalf of refugees and immigrants to the United States. Jolie has gone on dozens of missions to visit refugees and to provide support for those in need, and her message is true: "All of us would like to believe that if we were in a bad situation someone would help us." Her visit was encouraging for our team, and Jolie is innovative in how she uses her celebrity to support refugees.

I share Jolie's ongoing goal of increasing immigration to the United States, and her encouragement is welcome in large, complicated organizations. Achieving this goal requires innovation, and **innovation** is the product of collaborative relationships that mobilize creativity to generate value.

When Jolie came to visit the State Department, I was a newly appointed leader who was supporting the work of a great leader, Under Secretary Uzra Zeya. I did not yet have relationships with the career employees of the State Department. However, I started to meet my coworkers, and I began to actively listen and build on their ideas. Together, we generated new solutions to serve refugees under our Bureau of Population, Refugees, and Migration (PRM).

Under President Biden's policy direction, the United States government significantly increased the number of refugees it admitted, from only 11,411 in 2021 to 60,014 in 2023. It also increased its cap on refugee admissions, from 62,500 a year to 125,000. Those numbers represent safety and belonging for people who are fleeing persecution in their home countries. In addition, the Biden administration launched an innovative new refugee resettlement program, Welcome Corps (described in Practice 8: Innovation).

Innovation and immigration are deeply linked in this country. A 2022 study from the National Bureau of Economic Research found that immigrants drive business innovation in the United States. According to the study, immigrants make up 16 percent of all the inventors in this country, and they "produced 23 percent of total innovation output, as measured by number of patents, patent citations, and the economic value of these patents." Another 2022 study, this one from the National Foundation for American Policy, found that 55 percent of the founders of billion-dollar companies in the United States had at least one immigrant founder. Hamdi Ulukaya of Chobani, Sergey Brin of Google, and Pierre Omidyar of eBay are three examples of immigrant entrepreneurs.

In my position at the State Department, I provided leadership for the outreach to mayors and local elected officials. The responsibility for welcoming immigrants and refugees starts in local communities, and the State Department aimed to assist mayors—as well as individuals working in civil society and in private sectors—in the work of creating communities of belonging.

In this capacity, I joined State Department leaders at the Cities Summit of the Americas in Denver, Colorado. For me, this conference location had a special meaning. Denver was the place my family lived when we first arrived in the United States. Since that time, I had become a global leader, building relationships with mayors from around the hemisphere to develop innovative cross-sectional approaches to welcome immigrants.

Immigration, especially the status of refugees, remained a personal issue for me. At times, I was inundated with emails from potential immigrants who had been denied access to the United States. I worked with my colleagues to help resolve these issues. I got upset by the mistreatment of refugees. When the war broke out between Ukraine and Russia, African refugees who were attempting to flee Ukraine faced discrimination. Some countries neighboring Ukraine refused to welcome African refugees who had been studying and working in Ukraine.

I pushed the United States government to call, publicly and forcefully, for equal treatment for all refugees, regardless of their race, religion, or ethnicity. I was proud when the State Department announced that the

United States would cooperate with other agencies and governments to ensure equal treatment of refugees leaving Ukraine. And I was grateful when, only a month later, the president of the United States traveled to Poland to visit those refugees.

My Strengths as a Face of U.S. Foreign Policy

Every day in my role, I strived to represent the United States. When I was talking with international leaders, I was a diplomat; I communicated the Biden administration's priorities. When I was talking with leaders within the country from the sectors of government, business, and nonprofits, I was a political appointee; I listened to the voices of the public. As I served in both these roles, many people were surprised to see a Black, Muslim, Somali refugee acting as an official representative of the United States.

While my background and experience were not what many expected from someone representing the U.S.'s foreign policy, I knew that diversity was an asset in my leadership. Knowing my strengths, I centered my leadership on my talents and the aspects of my identity that make me unique. This **asset**-based approach was made easier by my serving under a leader like Under Secretary Uzra Zeya. As a woman and a child of immigrants from India, Uzra found strength in her diverse experiences. Uzra had spent much of her career in the State Department, so she was a wonderful boss and guide as I navigated the agency. Together, we promoted democracy in our conversations with political, business, and civil-society leaders from across the world and within the U.S.

In my two years at the State Department, I met with cross-sector leaders from sixty-five different countries. Many of the leaders I met shared about the challenges and opportunities for democracy in their countries. People questioned me too: including asking how a Somali refugee could represent American foreign policy. I remember a woman from Kenya approaching me in tears. She was inspired to meet me:

someone who, like her, was from East Africa, and had become a leader in President Biden's administration.

Under the leadership of Under Secretary Uzra Zeya, we always listened to the voices of the American people. We reached out beyond traditional Beltway stakeholders and sought leaders from across the country to contribute to the Summit for Democracy. I reached out to leaders in nearly every state in the country, to engage with those in leadership positions at a local level. Our leadership connected over 1,800 organizations with invitations to participate in the Summit for Democracy's Year of Action process.

I also organized an official visit to Minneapolis, Minnesota, for Under Secretary Zeya. Over two days, Uzra participated in community conversations with mayors, and with business and philanthropic leaders. Global Minnesota hosted an evening forum where Uzra provided a keynote address about the cause of global democracy to two hundred local leaders. I was humbled by the success of this visit, and I was grateful for the opportunity to bring together the strengths of my federal leadership and my local networks.

LEADING WITH TEAMS: INCLUSION, EMPATHY, AND DIGNITY

Investing in Equity across the World

At the invitation of Antony Blinken, secretary of state, I joined a reception in recognition of Eid al-Fitr at Blair House, a venue for diplomacy and the official guesthouse of the president. Secretary Blinken shared the podium with Alia Saleeban, a senior biology major at Howard University and president of the college's Muslim Students Association. To hear from both the Secretary of State—the highest-ranking member of the president's cabinet—and from a young Somali American woman was a highlight for me. I left the celebration with hope for a better future.

Inclusion occurs when leaders embrace collective belonging and mutual dignity. Inclusion welcomes new people and invests in new ideas. When inclusive leadership is working, new opportunities are born from relationships of empathy and respect. Inclusion in action can often be hard to identify, but when I see youth, like Alia, elevated to leadership, I see that something new is possible. It feels exciting, like sharing good work.

As a senior advisor for equity and inclusive democracy, I led the establishment of the first under-secretaria-wide DEIA (Diversity, Equity, Inclusion, and Accessibility) council at the U.S. State Department. Secretary Blinken recognized my unique contributions with a personal note of appreciation highlighting my role in helping leverage funding from the Office of the Undersecretary for Civilian Security, Democracy, and Human Rights to add a new leadership position for the first time ever, the Special Representative for Racial Equity and Justice. Building on my experience in philanthropy, I helped launch an innovation fund through the diplomatic programming fund of the U.S. State Department, where I led the selection of projects for funding that advance inclusion and belonging. Over twenty projects were funded within embassies and domestically.

Inclusive democracies must stand together in times of crisis. When over 20 million people were at risk of starvation in the Horn of Africa due to the worst drought in over forty years, the United States committed $361 million to the region. Vice President Kamala Harris also announced over $7 billion in private sector and U.S. government commitments to promote climate resilience, adaptation, and mitigation across Africa as part of the commitment from the U.S.-Africa Leaders Summit.

I could continue to list many ways that I supported inclusion at the State Department, but I want to return to the leadership of youth. I encouraged youth participation in the Summit for Democracy (described in the section on Biden's Presidential Initiative for Democratic Renewal in Practice 6: Inclusion). I organized recruitment events to encourage diverse groups of young people to consider careers in the State Department. Under Secretary Uzra Zeya shared about her inspiring thirty-year career with students and young adults in Denver, Minneapolis, New York, and Boston. In Minneapolis, I reconnected with Aashay Desai, a student at the University of Minnesota who had interned at the State Department with me. A business student and the son of immigrants from India, Aashay aspires to be a lawyer. When I make time to dialogue with new leaders about new ideas, I renew my purpose and maintain hope for the future.

Coming Together to Address Discrimination

I have never before worked at a place that faced more challenges in fostering a culture of inclusion. I worked with hundreds of good people who respected each other and strove to do good, but the State Department is historically known to have a deep culture of exclusion, given that it's one of the oldest federal departments. My empathetic leadership was tested by the continuous stories of colleagues who struggled to be valued.

As a leader, I was committed to genuinely caring about my colleagues' well-being. To have **empathy** is to understand, be sensitive to, or be aware of the feelings, thoughts, and experiences of others. I listened, without judgment, and I took the time to understand the diverse lived experiences of my colleagues. As a result, my team taught me about organizational culture. I established meaningful connections. I offered support. I cultivated strong relationships. As much as I could, I tried to create an environment where team members felt a sense of purpose and connection to a larger mission. I was grateful to have a lot of support in return.

Facing Challenges to Human Dignity

Dignity acknowledges the humanity of people. It is the first step in an authentic connection with another. The identity of individuals and groups of individuals must be recognized, no matter who they are. Before a person can be truly heard and seen, before they can become an equal partner, they need to receive respect.

When the president and vice president acknowledged my leadership with an appointment to a senior role, I experienced their respect. And I was not alone in this. They appointed dozens of Muslim Americans to political positions in the Biden-Harris administration. No other leaders of the United States have done more to elevate the leadership of Muslim Americans. I am especially aware that Vice President Kamala Harris has been thoughtful about developing relationships with Muslim presidential appointees. I joined a gathering that she hosted for Muslim American appointees at the Navy steps, at the Eisenhower Executive Office Building.

Their treatment of Muslim Americans is a significant improvement over that of Donald Trump, the previous president, who targeted Muslims for discrimination. His loud voice encouraged hatred of Muslims and of communities who are constantly under threat because of who they are. FBI data shows that anti-Muslim hate crimes spiked beginning in 2016, which corresponded with his Islamophobic campaign rhetoric.

One of Donald Trump's most Islamophobic actions was implementing a Muslim travel ban. At a rally on the campaign trail, he called for "a total and complete shutdown of Muslims entering the United States." As a result of his subsequent policies, over seventy-nine thousand Muslims with visas to travel to the United States were rejected. This ban prevented businesspeople, college students, and family members who were seeking reunification from coming to the United States.

The first travel ban included the countries of Iran, Libya, Somalia, Sudan, Syria, and Yemen—all Muslim-majority countries. He later added Nigeria, Eritrea, Sudan, Tanzania, Kyrgyzstan, and Myanmar. All these countries have significant Muslim populations, and the Rohingya people, from Myanmar, were fleeing genocide. In a feeble attempt to disguise the discrimination of the travel ban, Venezuela and North Korea were added to the list, but Donald Trump's words showed that his real intent was to block Muslims.

The Muslim travel ban was ended as a result of the people electing a new president. Muslims increased their political power and representation by helping to elect a new president. And in 2023, a national policy against Islamophobia was announced by President Biden and Vice President Harris: the U.S. National Strategy to Counter Islamophobia in the United States. Government is messy work. It involves passionate arguments, disagreements, and compromise. But it is also a place for transformational leadership. I am grateful to the president and vice president for encouraging my leadership and for making this country a place where the dignity of people of every kind of faith—or no faith at all—can be respected.

LEADING FROM SELF: ACCOUNTABILITY, PURPOSE, AND INTEGRITY

Transforming Leadership for Impact

When President Biden appointed me as a senior advisor, I established goals for my federal service. My acceptance of the role was a direct response to the new president's call to action to protect and promote democracy. My first goal was to advance his Presidential Initiative for Democratic Renewal. This agenda included new strategies to protect and promote democracy at home and abroad. I intended to bring my lived and professional experiences to that work, to see to it that when the administration talked about democracy, their vision was of an inclusive democracy. I would work to ensure that those affected by government policies and actions were included in decision-making.

As a leader, I must be **accountable** for my goals. When sharing these goals with my supervisor and coworkers, I invited them to help hold me accountable. I asked them to speak directly to me about my goals at any point when they were unsure of my actions: either the reason why I was doing something or whether the action itself was a good one. And they did.

My friends and family were also aware of my goals. I often sought their advice when I felt unsure about what to do, or when my goals seemed to conflict with each other. During my two years at the State Department, I made time to reflect on my achievements. Even before going to Washington, DC, I regularly used the beginning of a new year to reflect on the past months and to create goals for the following year. For the most important projects, I established quarterly goals, and I organized personal retreats that I used to hold myself accountable.

I hope this conclusion to the book clearly demonstrates the many accomplishments that came out of these years of federal service. It has been an honor to join with other public servants at the State Department and the White House to help America live out its ideals of building a multiethnic and multiracial democracy that protects everyone.

Along with my peers, I have provided a new face for American diplomacy and global leadership. Democratic renewal requires new images, symbols, and nuanced stories, and a new cadre of diverse leaders: including people who have lived and experienced global trauma. In this work, I have served as an example of the promise of democracy. It was democracy that enabled me to go from a refugee camp to representing America. It is my greatest hope that my example, and the examples set by those who came before and after me, can remind us all of the powerful impact everyone's vote and voice has on democracy.

Accountability is not only about evaluating the past. Accountability also involves having conversations about the future—and having such conversations and reflecting on my presidential appointment helped me see the power I have as a person, beyond being a symbol. I have learned many leadership lessons over my lifetime, and these lessons became clearer through my being accountable for my goals. In my leadership roles, I saw that the world needed more leaders, more voices who promote transformational leadership that advances the goals of inclusion, prosperity, and peace, achieved through empathy, innovation, and democracy. Through accountability, I refined the twelve leadership practices that form this book.

As I continue to advocate for democracy, I establish new goals for my leadership. As a reader of this book, you are a partner in my future. I invite you to reflect on your goals and to commit to being a leader for democracy. I also invite you to join me, to hold me accountable, as I train current and aspiring leaders in transformational leadership; my goal is to train over ten thousand people through my leadership framework in the next decade.

I also commit to be a leader for peace and prosperity in Africa. The continent of Africa plays a prominent role in promoting democracy. In my travels to Africa and in my DC experience, I have noted an absence of authentic and amplified voices speaking for Africa-U.S. global relations. A strengthened Africa-U.S. relationship is critical for inclusive global democracy, and my leadership can advance this goal. (In Practice 7: Assets, I wrote about the implementation of the U.S.-Africa Leaders Summit and the African Diaspora Council.) I want to build the nexus between Africa and the international community, and to help deliver freedom, opportunity, and prosperity for all. My commitment is to continue to be an agent for authentic relationship-building, so that I can help to advance inclusive democracy and economic prosperity. I will help form partnerships and facilitate exchanges of research and knowledge, experiences, and leadership development.

Leadership Conversations as a Hometown Diplomat

The **purpose** of my life is bigger than my job. When I left my home in Minnesota to serve in the Biden-Harris administration, I tried to stay in contact with those friends back home whose insights helped me discover my purpose. For help in staying true to that purpose, I have looked to those friends with whom I have worked to build an equitable economy and inclusive democracy. I have also helped them be true to themselves.

It is difficult to stay in touch from a distance. I experienced this not only as the demands in my life increased but also as the demands in my friends' lives did. In an attempt to stay connected to these friends and to my purpose, I applied to the Department of State's Hometown Diplomats Program, and I was accepted. Employees participating in the program are permitted to publicly share about their lives and careers, and about how the State Department's work impacts American communities. By becoming a hometown diplomat, I gained the opportunity to visit community organizations, and to build connections between the federal government and community leaders.

As a hometown diplomat, I gathered with Somali community leaders to participate in a community conversation on leadership. I returned to the Gale Mansion, a venue in Minneapolis, in May 2023, where I enjoyed a dinner in my honor, warm appreciative speeches, and cultural dances from young people. After an intermission, I was interviewed in front of an audience in the Somali language, and I was able to share leadership lessons and insights about my work. There were 180 people in the room, and the conversation was also livestreamed on local Somali television. This successful conversation became a model for three additional public leadership conversations I would have three months later in Somalia, during my travels there.

In May 2023, I joined my friend Tom Friedman for a lively panel discussion on the "Future of Work, Future of Schools." Organized by Dana

Mortenson, my friend who is the founder of World Savvy (described in Practice 11: Democracy), the gathering of two hundred people in Minneapolis examined how K–12 schools can best prepare young people for the future. I encouraged educators to focus on empathy, inclusion, and democracy as a foundation for learning, and as the way to transform intangible challenges into tangible solutions.

I also shared that education should be lifelong in nature and that it can occur in surprising places. For example, I attribute a lot of my career success to my first job at McDonald's. As a teenager and a refugee, I found that tasks that were simple to most were hard for me. But I learned to do them. An equitable economy requires points of access for people with no degree who can do an outstanding job to succeed. My job at McDonald's provided that access to me.

In September 2023, Minnesota Governor Tim Walz and I welcomed Hamza Barre, the prime minister of Somalia, on an official visit to our state. On my travels to Somalia a few months before, I had been greeted by the prime minister, and I was glad to return that favor by welcoming him to Minnesota. I am so grateful to Governor Walz for encouraging my leadership. My federal appointment prevented me from participating in his successful reelection campaign with Lt. Governor Peggy Flanagan, but I am happy to continue to advise the governor and his team from time to time.

I also addressed a group of Afghan refugees and their advocates at Metropolitan State University in Saint Paul in the summer of 2023. These recent refugees participated in a community needs assessment for Afghan refugees that was modeled on my previous work with Tayo Consulting Group in the Somali community (described in Practice 7: Assets). These refugees engaged filmmaker James Christenson to work with Afghan youth to create short films that share their story. With them, James built on our experience of working together on narrative change during the *Rumee* project (described in Practice 10: Humility).

These few examples show the value of continuing the work for shared purposes as much as schedules allow. These gatherings allowed me to celebrate my friends as they fulfilled their purpose, and they reminded me of my purpose. The world is full of demands and opportunities. Sometimes I can lose track of my purpose. I am grateful for conversations and experiences that help me find strength and continue to lead.

My Commitment to My Family

After two years in Washington, DC, I left my presidential appointment to return to my family: my wife, Ikran, and our four children, Samia, Subeir, Sabrina, and Suhur. When I left the Biden administration, important work remained to be done, but there will always be work to do including helping reelect President Biden so the good work of the first term can be carried on in a second term. Some encouraged me to consider an appointment as deputy assistant secretary of state, but I returned home to be a person of **integrity**. I am a husband and a father, and I am committed to my wife and children. I missed the daily presence of my family, and they missed me.

Leadership is about integrity. When I adopted my father's prayer to be useful to society, my commitment was not only to world peace, global prosperity, and inclusion. Being a good husband and father is one of the most useful ways to lead. I want to be a transformative example to my children as they find their purpose, and this requires being near them.

When I first came to DC, it was in the middle of a unique year for my wife and children, who had gone to spend a year in Africa. As refugees, Ikran and I had wanted our children to experience East Africa. We wanted them to meet their extended family; to experience the region's culture, food, and traditions; and to find out more about themselves. We worried that our children might have become a little spoiled by the benefits of life in the United States; through this trip, they could learn more about the struggles that people face. In Africa, Ikran helped our children navigate a new educational system, and she helped me bridge the distance.

Maintaining the strength of our family during that time was challenging. We had to make extra efforts to be honest, to communicate expectations clearly, and to have patience with each other. When Ikran and our children returned to Minnesota, the kids were excited to return to their friends, teachers, and routines. I was excited to see them more. I remember the rush of emotion I felt when taking our eldest, Samia, to her first day of high school. During the summer, I organized extended visits to DC for my family, and when I traveled to them from Washington, I guarded our time together. On my visits, I would drive our children to school, activities, and appointments. I even took them skiing: a new activity for me.

Ikran provided great encouragement to all of us. She supported our children as they succeeded in school, and her support allowed me to pursue public service. My family and I still sacrifice much, but I pray that my example provides inspiration and strength to my children. However, whatever difference I make in my work, my impact as a leader ultimately will be shown as much through the lives my children lead as it will through my accomplishments. Transformative leadership shows up in the commitment that a leader makes to others.

SOURCES

Introduction

Maxwell, J. C. (2007). *The 21 Indispensable Qualities of a Leader: Becoming the Person Others Will Want to Follow.* HarperCollins Leadership.

Practice 2: Purpose

Winfrey, O. (2002, July). "What Oprah Knows for Sure about Life's Biggest Adventure." *O, The Oprah Magazine.* https://www.oprah.com/ spirit/what-oprah-knows-for-sure-about-lifes-biggest-adventure.

Practice 3: Accountability

McGee, J. (1917, April 11). [Letter from John McGee to U.S. Senator Knute Nelson]. Knute Nelson Papers. Minnesota Historical Society.

Practice 4: Dignity

Edmondson, A. C. (2018). *The Fearless Organization: Creating Psychological Safety in the Workplace for Learning, Innovation, and Growth.* John Wiley & Sons.

Hicks, D. (2013). *Dignity: Its Essential Role in Resolving Conflict.* Yale University Press. https://doi.org/10.12987/9780300263503.

Practice 5: Empathy

Biden, J. [@Potus]. (2022, March 26). *I visited Ukrainian refugees who have fled to Poland this afternoon. You don't need to speak the same language to feel the roller-coaster.* Twitter. https://twitter.com/POTUS/status/1507742896820264962?lang=en.

Bureau of African Affairs. [@AsstSecStateAF]. (2022, February 28). *The United States is coordinating with UN agencies and other governments to ensure every individual, including African students, crossing from Ukraine.* Twitter. https://twitter.com/AsstSecStateAF/status/1498406259569143808.

Sinar, E., Paese, M., Smith, A., Watt, B., & Wellins, R. (2016). "High-Resolution Leadership: A Synthesis of 15,000 Assessments into How Leaders Shape the Business Landscape." *Development Dimensions International.* https://media.ddiworld.com/research/high-resolution-leadership-2015-2016_tr_ddi.pdf.

Practice 6: Inclusion

Friedman, T. L. (2005). *The World Is Flat: A Brief History of the Twenty-First Century.* Farrar, Straus and Giroux.

Part III: Leading the Organization

Jobs, S. (2005, June 12). "'You've Got to Find What You Love,' Jobs Says." Stanford.edu. https://news.stanford.edu/2005/06/12/youve-got-find-love-jobs-says/.

Tokar, S. (2023, October 3). "What Is Organizational Leadership?" Southern New Hampshire University. https://www.snhu.edu/about-us/newsroom/business/what-is-organizational-leadership.

U.S. Department of Health and Human Services. (2021, July 7). *Cultural Respect.* National Institutes of Health. https://www.nih.gov/institutes-nih/nih-office-director/office-communications-public-liaison/clear-communication/cultural-respect.

Practice 7: Assets

Buckingham, M. (2019, January 14). "3 Proven Ways to Win at Work, Says World-Renowned Talent Expert." CNBC.com. https://www.cnbc.com/2019/01/14/marcus-buckingham-3-scientifically-proven-ways-to-win-at-work.html.

Rath, T. (2007). *StrengthsFinder 2.0*. Gallup Press.

Practice 9: Prosperity

Boschee, J. (2012, October 18). "The Heart and Soul of Social Enterprise," *Jerr's Journal (Core Values)*. https://socialent.org/index.php/jerrs-journal-individual-essays/.

Gadnis, A. (n.d.). "#MeetTheMB100—Ashish Gadnis, Co-Founder & CEO, BanQu." https://meaningful.business/meetthemb100-2020-ashish-gadnis-co-founder-ceo-banqu-inc/.

Nelson, P. (2015, August). *Wellstone, Paul (1944–2002)*. MNopedia. https://www.mnopedia.org/person/wellstone-paul-1944-2002.

PDI Technologies. (2023, April 26). *Report Finds Americans Willing to Pay More for Sustainable Products*. PDI Technologies, Inc. https://pditechnologies.com/news/consumers-willing-pay-more-sustainability/.

United Nations Industrial Development Organization. (n.d.). *What Is CSR?* UNIDO. https://www.unido.org/our-focus/advancing-economic-competitiveness/competitive-trade-capacities-and-corporate-responsibility/corporate-social-responsibility-market-integration/what-csr.

Vonnegut, K. (2005, May 16). "Joe Heller." *The New Yorker*.

Part IV: Leading the Community

Palmer, P. (1977). *A Place Called Community*. Pendle Hill Publications.

Practice 10: Humility

Brown, B. (2015). *Daring Greatly: How the Courage to Be Vulnerable Transforms the Way We Live, Love, Parent, and Lead.* Avery Books.

Frankl, V. E. (1992). *Man's Search for Meaning: An Introduction to Logotherapy.* 4th ed. Beacon Press.

Ganz, M. (2009). "What Is Public Narrative: Self, Us & Now" (Working Paper). http://nrs.harvard.edu/urn-3:HUL.InstRepos:30760283.

Practice 11: Democracy

Biden, J. R. (2023, September 28). Remarks by President Biden Honoring the Legacy of Senator John McCain and the Work We Must Do Together to Strengthen Our Democracy. Whitehouse.gov.

Douglass, F. (1857). Frederick Douglass Papers: Speech, Article, and Book File, -1894; Speeches and Articles by Douglass, -1894; 1857, Two Speeches by Frederick Douglass; One on West India Emancipation . . . and the Other on the Dred Scott Decision. [Manuscript/Mixed Material] Retrieved from the Library of Congress, https://www.loc.gov/item/mss1187900388/.

Greiner, L.E., & Schein, V.E. (1988). *Power and Organization Development: Mobilizing Power to Implement Change.* FT Press.

Practice 12: Peace

Annan, K. (2001, December 10). Nobel lecture. NobelPrize.org. nobelprize.org/prizes/peace/2001/annan/lecture/.

BlackPast. (2009, January 26). (1994) Nelson Mandela's Inaugural Address as President of South Africa. BlackPast.org. https://www.blackpast.org/global-african-history/1994-nelsonmandela-s-inaugural-address-president-south-africa/.

Economist Intelligence. (2022). *The Democracy Index.* https://www.eiu.com/n/campaigns/democracy-index-2022/.

International IDEA. (2021). *International Institute for Democracy and*

Electoral Assistance (IDEA) Annual Review 2021. https://www.idea
.int/2021-annual-review/home#message-from-leadership.

Lewis, C. S. (1971). *The Four Loves*. Mariner Books.

The Fund for Peace. (2022). *Fragile States Index Annual Report
2022*. https://fragilestatesindex.org/wp-content/
uploads/2022/07/22-FSI-Report-Final.pdf.

United Nations. (n.d.). *Engage: How to Deal with Hate Speech?* United
Nations. https://www.un.org/en/hate-speech/take-action/
engage#:~:text=Whenever%20possible%2C%20do%20not%20
remain,to%20back%20up%20your%20argument.

Conclusion

Gitlin. M. (2009). *Audrey Hepburn: A Biography*. Greenwood Biographies.

ABOUT THE AUTHOR

From child refugee to U.S. presidential appointee, Hamse Warfa has navigated some astonishing twists and turns. A passionate leader, he has more than twenty-five years of global leadership experience across federal and state governments, philanthropic organizations, and non-profits, and in the private sector as a successful tech entrepreneur. Warfa's mission is to inspire a more prosperous world by encouraging leaders to translate intangible organizational and societal challenges into tangible solutions and exponential impact. He accomplishes this by providing leadership strategy, training, and innovative leadership technology tools and content designed to accelerate impact.

In January 2022, President Biden appointed Warfa as his senior advisor to the U.S. State Department to advance a global democracy agenda, including the 2023 Summit for Democracy supported by seventy-four nations. Warfa received a State Department 2023 Meritorious Honor Award for innovation and advancing equity in the department's work. Prior to joining the federal government, Warfa was the deputy commissioner for Workforce Development at the Department of Employment and Economic Development in Minnesota. Appointed by Governor

Tim Walz in April 2019, Deputy Commissioner Warfa served as the highest-ranking African immigrant official in the Minnesota executive branch of government. In this position, he oversaw Minnesota's employment and training programs, the Office of Economic Opportunity, the state's fifty-one job centers, the Governor's Workforce Development Board, and the Office of Immigrant and Refugee Affairs.

In addition to his public-sector work, Warfa is an innovative and successful serial entrepreneur. He is the cofounder and executive vice president at BanQu Inc., a software company selected for an MIT Innovation award and recognized by the Obama administration as a leader in its field. He also founded Tayo Consulting Group, which helps philanthropic clients refine their goals and identify program activities to fund.

Prior to his entrepreneurial endeavors, Warfa worked as a senior program officer at Margaret A. Cargill Philanthropies, leading the organization's domestic and international children and families grant programs.

Warfa holds a master's in organizational management and leadership from Springfield College in Massachusetts, as well as a bachelor of arts in political science from San Diego State University. He also completed executive education at Harvard Business School as part of the Young American Leaders Program. He is a 2016 Bush Foundation Fellow, a recipient of the 2017 Minnesota Facing Race Award, and an Ashoka Global Fellow for his social entrepreneurship work. Warfa is the author of *America Here I Come: A Somali Refugee's Quest for Hope* and the producer of an upcoming documentary film based on his book.